Praise for *running with slugs*

Eric Arnold's *running with slugs* captures the adolescent experience with all of its absurdities, profundities, epiphanies and angst. In Kro Kandle, the book's thirteen-year-old protagonist and narrator, Mr. Arnold has created an American 'Adrian Mole.' Kro Kandle is searching for meaning while navigating through the rough terrain of middle school. This book is a must read for all teachers, parents, counselors, therapists and, of course, all middle school students.

> —Fred Lown, retired middle school teacher and author of
> *Langston Hughes: An Interdisciplinary Biography* and co-author
> of *Reading and Writing Poetry with Teenagers*

This delightful story has something for everyone – adventure, magic, and even a hint of mystery. *running with slugs* takes readers on a journey that bounces happily from silly to serious, from playful to profound.

> —Quinn D. Eli, playwright, educator and author of *Homecoming:*
> *The Story of African-American Farmers*

running with slugs

the *official* handbook for living in a world surrounded by slugs

Eric Arnold

A great book to do an easy book report,
book talk or book share on
but the book could be more than that—
just don't tell anyone.
Or everyone.

Joseph –
To a master story
teller~ The world is
hungry for more.
And, to a good friend~
Eric Arnold
1/19

Warning to English teachers! *Don't Read This Book* and, please, don't ever assign it to your
class to read.

First Edition

Paperback ISBN: 978-1-62720-157-5

Printed in the United States of America

Design by Apprentice House
Cover art by Shelby Ehret
Author photo by Ilene Perlman
Development by Alexandra Chouinard

Published by Apprentice House

Apprentice
House Press
Loyola University Maryland

Apprentice House
Loyola University Maryland
4501 N. Charles Street
Baltimore, MD 21210
410.617.5265 • 410.617.2198 (fax)
www.ApprenticeHouse.com
info@ApprenticeHouse.com

A man's got to take a lot of punishment to write a really funny book.

—Ernest Hemingway

This book
is
divided
into the four

sometimes full,
sometimes empty

Chambers of the Heart

and

is not dedicated to English teachers who make kids hate
everything about English class especially having to read
a book in class.

Like this one.

Prologue: A useful checklist before the book starts—

Slug: A Definition

Mostly in human form.
All ages/shapes/sizes/forms
It takes lifeblood from you.
It takes life-air from you.
It will do anything to keep you from being you.
Or from you finding out who you are. Or aren't.
Or could be.

Book Dedication before the Official Book Dedication

This book *is* dedicated to the *kids* who have *slug* English teachers. (BTW, English teachers are sometimes called ELA/English Language Arts: They can run but they can't hide.)

And even if you are homeschooled for "English class", this book is for you. No way can you get out of this!

And, just so you know, slug teachers teach *any* subject, not just English.

This is important.

Any subject can qualify.

And any teacher can qualify, too.

Students can be slugs, too—probably no surprise there, but more on that later.

You know who you are if you have a slug teacher. Just read this book.

I know you will understand and I hope this book helps. It certainly can't hurt.

And, no book should hurt, really, unless your slug English teacher makes you read it and destroys it not only for you and your class but for your whole life because you will never want to read a book again, especially if you don't have to.

So, if you can and you have to, make reading this book a "good one," okay?

And, good luck.

Especially if you have a slug-infested-and-carried-via-boogers-through-her-nasal-passages English teacher like Mrs. (don't call me *Ms.*) Pencey who not only makes you outline what the plot of the book is frontward but she also makes you outline what the plot of the book is backwards.

Or, she says that the theme of every novel can be summed up in one noun.

Imagine that someone's whole life can be summed up in one noun.

One *noun*!

If this is the first and last book you will ever read on your own, I'll try to help as much as I can.

And if you want to use this book for a book report, a book talk, a book share, or whatever you have to call it for *your* Mrs. Pencey, I will help as much as I can. Just never choose to live a *slug's life*. Never. You never have to just because everyone around you is.

Because *almost* everyone around you is. You can survive the slugs around you and find those who aren't.

That's why I am writing this book.

Me. Kro.

Kro Kandle.

Age 13.

A Non-Journal

This book is not a journal.

It drives me crazy when people write books in fake journal form. By my estimation, only one-eighth of one-half percent of the world's population keeps a journal, anyway, so this book is for the rest of us.

And, it's for them, too.

I don't discriminate against those fourteen people in the world who keep a journal.

Because, if you're reading this book, I know that you've been through enough in life already since you *live in a world surrounded by slugs.*

This is *my* book and I purposely wrote it not in a *journal form* because I don't keep a journal.

I never have and I never will.

When I do have ideas, I write them down on a scrap piece of paper and I stuff them in an empty pickle jar and I look at them and think about them. Some of those ideas made it into this book and some of them will stay with me.

But, most of them are here.

Most of them are about everyday things that I think about.

Maybe you do, too. Depends on the *slug climate* where you live.

A Non-Memoir/Blog/Tweet

Definition of a memoir: A memoir is, basically, an autobiography. You know, when someone, actually, writes their *own* biography, their own life story. Sometimes it's a person's *whole* life so I'm not sure why it is not called an autobiography.

Sometimes it's just a *certain* part or parts of someone's life that was a highlight, a challenge or a hard time that a person would rather forget but instead he or she is sharing it with the world.

Go figure.

Examples: 1) *My Life Bagging Groceries after School: From Paper to Plastic to EcoBags;* 2) *Growing Up in a Petri Dish: I was the Daughter of a Middle School Science Teacher.*

This book is not a memoir. Everyone thinks their life is so stupidly interesting that they have to write a memoir about it or from it.

Writing about the experience of trying to survive living in a family surrounded by a slug parent/aunt/uncle could be considered a memoir.

Or, if I were writing about how I survived my mostly slug-infested Hapworth Middle School with a slug social studies teacher wanting to know the gossip of who was dating *whom* or a slug PE teacher who thinks that *teaching* is opening the door to the gym and throwing a ball in the middle of the floor and then texts his friends on the "outside" while the students are engaged in unsupervised *mayhem* (such rich vocabulary) on the gym floor and groups of mostly girls, I don't know why, are sitting in the bleachers talking.

About what?

Who knows or cares.

But, somehow, it becomes everyone's business.

Somehow.

But this book is not a memoir because it is happening now.

And it could be happening to you.

No matter who your teachers or parents or guardians are.

Or aren't.

Or who you are.

Or aren't.

A not so mental note to English teachers about assigning a memoir project for their class: Don't, unless it's about a non-slug person.

Except who will be the judge? Sometimes a person can be slug and non-slug.

You might have to wear slug-glasses to find out.

And, this is not a *blog*.

It's not a giant *tweet*.

It's a *book*!

And, that's important.

Very.

Non-Slug Teachers

Rare. They are very rare.

They are almost extinct in many schools.

You will know when you have a non-slug teacher.

Having just *one* can help.

Breathing in class, for one, is easier.

That makes *life* easier, too.

I was lucky: I had two (amazing, I know!)—Mr. Bloom/seventh-grade English, Ms. Chen/a take-no-prisoners-guidance counselor and she's not even really a teacher.

And, I'll throw in Ms. Kazakh/Latin teacher. Well, she's almost there.

That's about three. My Mt. Rushmore of non-slug teachers minus one.

And if I'd had Ms. Ibraheem, the non-slug science teacher, I would have a Mt. Rushmore royal flush of four but no such luck.

It's a short list. Very short.

Maybe I'll put my dad in there as the fourth non-slug teacher.

That I was able to find just three or four non-slug teacher types is very lucky.

Bordering on miracle.

Non-Slug Family

Pretty rare, as well.

Sometimes medium rare.

And, if you are a truly daily-kissed-by-the-gods kind of person and, amazingly, if you're maybe from a family nearing some kind of *normalcy*, whatever that is, and, luckily, have at least one non-slug parent or guardian who may be left-handed, gay, straight, trans, cis, fluid, non-binary, plays guitar, repairs cars and specializes in mufflers, is a secretly meat-loving vegan, collects old thermometers and Shakespeare love sonnets, never irons, makes pizza from scratch, dyes hair in orange polka dots and wears matching shorts, knows computers, knits or is not even a parent or guardian but is an uncle, an aunt or, even, a parental-type figure like a, gasp, teacher, not legally or socially related or, even, again, some adult in your imagination, then you need words.

Non-Slug Friends

Get some.

Hold on to them.

They are hard to find.

Do a magical dance to get one or some.

Do a magical dance and be yourself.

Be yourself.

Non-Slug Words and Others

If you speak words, you might as well like them.

And, if you speak or text at least ten words a day, you might as well read some, too, like in a book.

And, hopefully, these words that I am writing you'll read.

For you and *me*.

Not "I."

Thanks, Mr. Bloom.

Author's Note: Sometimes there might be a non-slug teacher who escapes my *slug radar*. It happens. Be on the lookout wherever you are.

The Official Book Dedication

This book is dedicated to the writer and adventurer—
Ernest Hemingway

Ernest Hemingway was asked to write a eulogy to be read at a funeral
for his friend, Gene Van Guilder.

Gene was duck hunting.
He was accidentally shot to death.
The year 1939.

Ernest died twenty-two years later.
Shot to death.
The year 1961.

Those words that Ernest wrote for his friend also said a lot about his own life.
Some of those words from that eulogy now appear on his own memorial where he is buried not
too far from Gene in Idaho.

Here are those words:
Best of all he loved the fall
The leaves yellow on the cottonwoods
Leaves floating on the trout streams
And above the hills
The high blue windless skies
Now he will be a part of them forever

Ernest Hemingway
Born: July 21, 1899, in Oak Park, Illinois.
Many starts, stops, places and pages in between on his way to becoming a man.
Died: July 2, 1961, in Ketchum, Idaho.

**Part One
of
the
Four Chambers
of
the
Heart**

—The Left Atrium—

"Write a Book"

My aim is to put down on paper what I see and what I feel in the best and simplest way.

—Ernest Hemingway

Meet Ernest

Ernest Hemingway made me write this book.

He did.

No, he's not some unlucky kid whose parents ran out of good names and came up with *Ernest*.

And he's not some kid who sits behind me in math class looking on my paper for the right answers.

And, if he were trying to cheat off of me, good luck to him.

Living in a World Surrounded by Slugs Rule: *Never cheat off of someone who is more of a slacker than you, not as smart as you or who just hates the class!*

I hate math.

More than anything.

There is only one right answer in math and I never think there is one right answer.

To anything.

I got off the math track at *arithmetic*.

And I never looked back or forward.

That was enough for me.

Addition and subtraction and division and multiplication.

The Four Mathematical Functions.

And its subdivision:

Long division.

Short division.

Divide.

And conquer.

Me.

Sit and Stand.

Up or Down.

Win/Lose.

More or Less.

The only numbers I like are on money, addresses, phone numbers, ages (mine), shoe sizes, sports scores, height (mine but the numbers aren't getting very big so far), computer upgrades, music rankings, trivia questions and answers (Do you know the ten events in the decathlon?), days remaining in school, days remaining to my birthday, my birthday, days in a row that my mother wasn't just plain unfunny, weather reports and credit cards.

As if I had one of those.

Hardly.

So, who is Ernest?

That's a good question and I'll tell you.

Anyway, you'll need to know for this book.

And to know about my life you'll need to know something about his.

I got his name from my English teacher, Mr. Bloom. "Kro, here's a writer I think you'll like. He had a really interesting life and, like you, didn't suffer fools gladly."

A compliment from a teacher can go a long way.

Especially if it's a teacher that you like and is also of the non-slug variety.

Ernest was a famous American writer and adventurer who was originally from Illinois.

He wrote books and short stories and was married **four** times. He had a moustache and sometimes a beard.

And he loved Spain.

¿Que pasa?

He did everything: drove an ambulance in World War I and got wounded and was decorated for heroism.

And he was a journalist.

He traveled to Africa and lived in Cuba for a while.

He liked sports like skiing, bullfighting, mountaineering, fishing, hunting and boxing.

These sports are hard to come by in my neighborhood.

He was not shy about what he liked.

Or thought was important.

The man had opinions.

"There are only three sports," Ernest once wrote, "bullfighting, horse racing, and mountaineering; all the rest are merely games."

Don't worry—it's not time to throw away your lacrosse stick or catcher's mitt—yet.

Ernest had definite ideas about things.

And experiencing things.

Some, most and all things.

And that's what is interesting about him.

He wasn't afraid of both—ideas and experiences.

That appeals to me, too, and I'm only thirteen and an eighth-grader at Hapworth Middle School.

And sometimes you read something that can change your life.

I think I did just that.

I read somewhere that Ernest wrote that there are *Four Things to Do to Be a Man*.

So I looked for them everywhere.

And I finally found it.

Although there is no real proof that he actually said this.

Or wrote this.

I believe he did.

The *Four Things to Do to Be a Man* makes sense to me.

Mostly.

Ernest certainly lived life to the fullest on his own terms and he might not be the perfect example of what it means to be a man and I'm not even sure what it means to be a man.

He did drink too much and from what I read, he was not a great dad.

It's complicated.

Nobody is perfect.
Not even you.
And not even me.
Although it's hard for me to say that.
Not your principal.
School counselor.
Sometimes called guidance counselor.
Your teachers.
Next door neighbor.
Your best friend.
Your parent.
Or two.
Or three.
Or four.

But I first learned from him what it takes to be a man.
Or, at least he started me thinking about it.
It was time.
And I owe Ernest thanks for this.

The first thing to do to be a man according to Ernest was to write a book.
And that's what I am doing.
Right here.

I'm writing a book.
This book.

Me

I'm not a man—yet.
I've got to figure out the how-to-be-a-man plan from Ernest, first.
That's what this book is about.

And, it's not finished yet.
So, I can't be a man.
Yet.
And, after this, there are three other things I must do to become a man.
According to Ernest.
And, because I agree, according to me.

I'm not tall and I'm not that short.
That wasn't my plan.
I'm sure DNA had something to do with it.
Waiting for my growth spurt.
I'm thinking any day now.
Why not?

I'm Kro Kandle.
Dark hair. Long.
Even when the style is to have it short.
I like it long. It's the Ernest in me.

Olive skin.
My mother says I look good in rich, gem colors.
I look good in anything near my bed that I can find in the morning.
If it's clean, that's a plus.
The smell test is usually accurate.
Does it really matter?

She's descended from a long line of New Hampshire Yankees.
Not the baseball kind but more of the "We almost came over on the Mayflower but there were no more seats available and we weren't cool enough so we couldn't get a boarding pass" type.
On my dad's side, well, he says that we're descended from a long line of horse thieves in Eastern Europe.
I know. What a pedigree from both sides but somehow it works for me.
Somehow.

I'm athletic.
And stereotyped into all of the positions in sports for smaller fast guys.
Baseball: second base or short stop. Basketball: point guard.
Football: halfback or safety. No tackling, please. I don't want to be tackled by Gandolph goons so I only play touch in the neighborhood.

And, I want to make sure I reach my growth spurt.
Alive.
And with limbs.

Soccer: midfielder. I've got more moves than a can of worms. Well, I think I do.
I think I have a vision of the field so I can pass the ball to a teammate. In middle school soccer, though, no one is really ready for or anticipating a pass.
It looks good, though, to pass.
Or to even look around so it looks like you are going to pass.

Haven't played lacrosse:
Yet.
Too much equipment.
I'm kind of a choose-a-sport-that-requires-as-little-equipment-as-possible-kind-of-guy.
I mostly think I would like lacrosse, though, because I like the short version of lacrosse—
LAX.
That can be me, too—LAX.

Addict

That's me, too.
Just like Ernest.
I guess I am like him in a way.
More than I thought.

For him, it was alcohol.
For me?
Chips.

Potato.
All kinds of chips—salsa, ranch, salt and vinegar, kettle, original, with salt,
without salt, ...
You name it. If it's a potato chip, I'm for it.

I'm always *jonesing* for chips.

School lunches don't help.
The supposedly-healthy-and-improved-and-good-for-you school lunches.
Kids just buy lunch and trade the dessert for chips that other kids bring from home.
Kids bring a lunch from home and trade the dessert for chips.

My standard lunch: two bags of chips, a cookie and you're out.
Once a year I add something green—St. Patrick's Day cookies.

I'm trying to get off the chips thing.
You know, the whole athlete thing.
Or wannabe athlete thing.

Not there with the chips thing yet.
Not rushing it, either.
Sort of going to zen with it.
Zen it happens, zen it will.

Okay, and pickles, too.
Half sours.
Dill, too.
Pickles and chips.
Tasty, Ernest?

Me. Poet/maybe.

Ode to Chips
A Limerick
Dedicated to All Chips Everywhere

There once was a boy who loved chips,
Who said, a good chip needs no dip.
Cool ranch, barbecue,
Sour cream, cheddar, too—
And flavors must meet on the lips!

—Kro Kandle

Another Limerick
Dedicated to NBA Dreams

There is a kool kid named "The Kro"—
His NBA dream is on hold.
Eighth grade is up first—
For better or worse.
With Ernest, he'll learn how to grow!

—Double K

Poetry

Seventh-grade English with Mr. Bloom.

A heavenly existence before the painful Mrs. Pencey, the eighth-grade English teacher from hell, who is the source of all that is wrong with the world: climate change, mandatory state testing of public school students on the reading comprehension of ridiculous stories and all of the wars in the world—past, present, future, on Earth and beyond—including all virtual and gaming wars.

I learned how to write poetry with Mr. Bloom and I thought I would hate it.

And I did.

At first.

Me.

A poet?

Still not sure.

Pain in the ass student for a slug teacher?

I'm your man.

Not man, yet, but you know what I mean.

Sloppy son who wears socks eight days in a row, at least, without changing them which drives a too-tidy mom nuts?

I'm your almost man.

Brother to a sister?

In name only.

Athlete?

In my dreams, mostly.

Sometimes on the field.

Traveling son who would rather live more with his dad than his mom and drink right out of the milk carton from the fridge?

When I drink milk.

That's me with a creamy milk moustache.

A friend to *The Three Alliterations* (More on "them/us" later . . .).

With pleasure.

But poet?

Maybe "In Training."

I fought the poetry urge tooth and nail.

Metaphor, there.

It didn't quite fit with my image as I am still constructing the image that I want to be.

Image in training.

"Do you listen to songs on the radio?" Mr. Bloom asked the class.

The class looked around as if here was another teacher question that required no answer. *The rhetorical question.*

The face of the giant clock on the wall is covered by a faded piece of orange construction paper so no one can stare at the clock all day. Mr. Bloom had someone write *Tempus fugit* on it.

"Well, do you?" Mr. Bloom wasn't backing down. He went from *rhetorical* to *real* pretty quick.

"You, Campy? Ever listen to a song on the radio? Ever?" he said with a quizzical look on his face. "Ever?"

Campy looked around. First, at me.

My expression? Go for it!

Then she looked at the third member of our *Three Alliterations*—Karlos. He gave her the same reaction and added a shrug.

A shrug can tell a lot.

Shrugs are good.

Campy, thinking she was stepping into a Mr. Bloom teacher trap designed to make a point, caved.

"Yes," she quietly said.

Mr. Bloom looked at her.

And, to the rest of the class.

We were all waiting for the point.

Mr. Bloom was getting that teacher-kind-of-excited-with-an-aha-moment-about-to-burst look on his face. "Then, you're also listening to poetry! Songs are poetry!"

My Consonant Trio looked at each other.

Okay, was the general consensus of the three of us and the rest of the class. We all liked Mr. Bloom but couldn't get to his level of excitement or interest with this one.

Back to Campy. "Okay," she said as she represented the class.

"Then," Mr. Bloom made a dramatic pause, "when you are listening to songs on the radio, you are also listening to poetry." Another dramatic English teacher pause. "Poetry."

I bought it.

So did Campy and Karlos.

The three of us, *The Three Alliterations*, as Mr. Bloom would call us, agreed.

But I was the only one of us three, it seems to me, who got the poetry bug.

Bad.

It does make me think.

Always.

Helps you look at this upside-down-low-hanging-slug-infested Earth.

There are exceptions.

And, it would've probably been easier to write this book as a poetry book.

I'm not saying that writing poetry is easier.

It's not.

It could, maybe, have been a shorter book, though, even with tons of poems.

Ernest in my head: "A man doesn't take the easy way out."
Okay. I'm writing a book.
In prose.
With poetry in it when I can.
I put raspberry jam poetry on my toast.
In the morning.

Whole wheat.

But I can't guarantee gluten-free rhymes.

Me. Poet/maybe.

My Poetry Head

Knows more
than my everyday head.
It seems.

Poetry
gets in—
and
goes out.

Differently.

It rushes in—

Screams out—

Storms out—

Runs out—

and keeps running—

Into words—
And me.

                    —Kro

Me. Poet/maybe.

Raspberry Poetry on Toast
in the Morning

In the morning.
Raspberry poetry on toast.
It starts me.
My day.

It clears my head
My thoughts.
It messes up my head
My thoughts.

It makes me laugh.
It doesn't make me cry
and
would I admit it if it did?
Or share it.

It can make sense.
And, not.
Or only to me.

It can rap, free verse and rhyme.
Sometimes at the same time.

It's always me.
Me.
It makes my day with
Raspberry poetry on toast
in the morning.

—K. Kandle

Me. Poet/maybe.

Radio

I can't sing.
I write songs.
I am a poet.
I write poems.
I sing.

—Kro Kandle

House(s)

Two is better than one.

Or so they say.

My dad lives in Cambridge, Massachusetts. Our house is a fifteen-minute walk to Harvard Square. If you are planning to be a runaway, that might be a good place to head to. Don't tell anyone, please, that it was my idea. Other runaways are there along with people looking for runaways so it probably isn't that great of an idea, really.

Stay suffering in middle school.

At least you're off the streets and the worst thing that can happen to you aside from losing any mental growth or stimulation is that you hear a bad teacher joke here or there and your classmates can't really tell if you are wearing your hair that way for "Crazy Hair Day" or if it's your normal style.

Oh, and your locker might get broken into.

And, since, no one really puts a lock on their locker, then is it really broken into?

And what would one want to steal? A ripped packet of three-hole loose-leaf paper without margin lines? Or, a cemetery-like pit of chewed up No. 2 pencils?

My dad lives in a two–family house and rents out the bottom half to a Dutch guy getting his Ph.D. in astrophysics at MIT and his wife who works in a bank. Claude wants to be an astronaut and explore the moon and his wife, Elke, wants to have a family on Earth. Hope they can figure it out.

Cambridge is like, well, probably, different than a lot of places.

First, there is Harvard University right there.

I know, duh, hence, and does anyone really ever speak the word *hence* out loud or is it one of those words that is only written down?

There are a lot of people who are trying to look smart, are smart, are rich, are rich and smart, are not that smart and rich and still at Harvard but still look rich and smart or, maybe, they are just hanging out in the 'Square' which is what people do at the Square.

Hang.

It wasn't a bad place to grow up assuming that I am finished growing up.

And if you like dead and stuffed skunks, aardvarks, moose and beetles, the Harvard Museum of Natural History has thousands of taxidermied animals. That was always a Saturday adventure looking at these animals—standing still, lifeless with bits of their hide rotting and tearing off. Okay, it was a little creepy looking at a dead grizzly bear or a duck-billed platypus.

Aren't all platypus, by nature, duck-billed?

Redundant.

Redundant.

Anyway, as long as one of the dead animals didn't move, I was okay.

After the museum, a trip to the center of the Square to watch street musicians, magicians and performers was next.

A guy balancing a shopping cart on his chin was always a highlight.

Mom.

Or "Mother" as she likes to be called.

She lives in Watertown, a town next to Cambridge.

In a too-tidy house.
Hospital quiet.
Not many signs of life in the house.
A dust bunny has a life span of, maybe, 2.3 seconds, there.
The Harvard Museum of Natural History might be interested for a future taxidermy project for an endangered species.
In that house.

That I ended up living there over half of the time is a mystery of life.
I'm not tidy.
I'm not quiet.
And my earliest career goal was to learn how to balance a lawn mower on my chin and work as a street performer in Harvard Square.
Okay, maybe not one of those rider mowers but one of those old-fashioned push mowers.

I never knew any of my grandparents on both sides of my family. Sad, really, because I heard cool stuff about all four although I'm sure I was only told the good stuff: a mechanic who could fix anything and even invented a screwdriver grip; one who was a super cook known for making everything from scratch and never from a box and having standing-room-only Thanksgiving dinners and the NFL games were allowed to be on TV during dinner; another who read two books a week without *having* to for any school assignment; one who was a swimmer who could beat anyone in her age bracket!
Weird that they died either before I was born or when I was too little to remember them. How can someone not be remembered? I blame it on me being a kid but more realistically, in my case, my babyhood. Is it my fault that I don't remember or didn't know them? I'm still figuring this one out.
Plus, none of them, as far as I can tell, were even slugs.
As far as I can remember.
Or so I've been told.

But four cool grandparents were replaced by my Auntie Melba and her almost husband, Uncle Dewey. They would drop in for a short or long period of time from up north in Claremont, New Hampshire.
Mostly uninvited.
Auntie Melba would hang her hand-washed oversized granny underwear over the shower curtains in the bathroom.
Not a pretty sight, as you can imagine.
Child abuse, in my book.
Who can I call?

Watertown Police: *What is your emergency?*
Kro Kandle: *Well, it's hard to explain. Some may think it's not an emergency but to a thirteen-year-old boy, worried about his growth spurt, it could be damaging to his . . .*
Watertown Police: *Can you be more specific?*
Kro Kandle: *Granny underwear. It's granny underwear. Two pairs.*

Watertown Police: *Now tell me what the exact problem is.*

Kro Kandle: *That they are there. In the bathroom. Larger than life and lifeless at the same time. A hand-rinsed parachute-sized pair of underpants hanging over the shower curtain, too!*

Watertown Police: *Understood. What's the address of the emergency?*

Kro Kandle: *It's the cleanest house in Watertown with the freshly swept and shampooed lawn.*

Watertown Police: *With whom am I speaking?*

Kro Kandle: *A victim, a victim of granny panty abuse. Another sad tale . . .*

Watertown Police: *What's the phone number I can call you back on?*

Kro Kandle: *It's too late . . . it's too late. They're back, they're home . . .*

Watertown Police: *Hello, hello! Sir, Sir . . . are you still there?*

Me. Poet/maybe.

Are Two Better?

Are two friends better than one?

Are two divorced parents better than some?

Are two houses better than none?

Are two wings better than one?

When do you know if you have already won?

—Kro Kandle

Sister

Chloe.
Nine years old.
Invisible.

Different generation.

Dinner at My Mother's

There are assigned seats at my mom's house and we eat dinner, never supper.

Dinner expectations can be interchangeable with instructions for standardized testing in school with some or very little variation:

Before you begin to eat, you need to know that all cell phones, electronic devices, music players and original thoughts must be turned off. You must not send and/or receive text messages or original thoughts either through your electronic devices or via your mind to someone else's. You must not make or receive calls or think of an idea that might make either a parent or sibling choke on a drumstick of originality or creativity during the dinner process. Please turn your cell phone and mind off and place both under your chair or I will hold them until after dinner or when your brain rots away from atrophy— whichever comes first.

HAND

Any second it could happen.

Each day I would try to predict what could, arguably, be one of the greatest natural disasters of all time to take place at Hapworth Middle School.

Karlos and me (okay, Mr. Bloom, you are in my still developing brain—Karlos and I), at the beginning of class, would write down on a piece of paper the exact time it could happen during HAND (Human and Nutrition Dynamics) class.

"Ten minutes into class, *guapo*, I'm sure of it!" Karlos would boast.

"No way. He's going to get a second wind and make it to the last five minutes and then it's all over. Then I'm going to make a mad run to the office and say we need a custodian in Room 121 pronto and, probably, a doctor, too!"

We'd do a fist bump and watch.

And, wait.

Wait for the moment of mass destruction of Mr. Basil, the world's most out of shape HAND teacher in, possibly, the world, who also wears bad novelty ties.

Author's Quick Note: Do other schools in the world even have a HAND class? Could students around the world be this lucky? If you do, it might be called something else.

Or, at least in the Northern Hemisphere.

A potential *Guinness World Records* holder teaching us about being healthy.

And, he was ready to implode in front of our very eyes—a moment of mass destruction with potentially popping corpuscles and veins and a splattering pool of blood all over the floor and walls. (Sorry—don't mean to be body shaming on Mr. Basil in the HAND section of my book. Not my intent. As a writer, I need to be a keen observer of everything around me and, besides, I'm on to a bigger metaphor, here.)

That's what would get me through HAND class.

And where I started to figure out and begin to learn, really, that adults can say one thing and mean another.

It was at the beginning of the formulation of my slug philosophy of Hapworth and, even, the world.

And I hadn't even met Ernest Hemingway yet.

Clearly, Mr. Basil has never met a box of Pop-Tarts that he didn't like.

Or not be able to snarf down a bucket of root beer ice cream at one sitting.

If there is even such a thing as root beer ice cream.

It doesn't matter.

He was teaching us HAND.

How to live a healthy lifestyle, how not to smoke, not to drink or take drugs and how to deal with stress in one's life.

Now that's ironic.

Irony: when you expect one thing and something else happens.

"Eat a green vegetable at every meal," he would bark at the end of each class while the students would bolt to the door for freedom. Nothing green has ever reached his mouth unless you count Doritos dipped in *salsa verde* for St. Patrick's Day. "Remember, there is a test tomorrow on adolescent lifestyles. Be ready!" How can I be ready? I'm living it even though you could say I'm still in early adolescence.

Karlos looked at me as he tried to join the class stampede by hurtling over Sarah Tsippi's massive stack of perfectly aligned and color coordinated binders on the floor. "It didn't happen today. Basil's head stayed in one piece. Not one vein popped and his forehead didn't crack open. Not even a nosebleed. No one wins."

Borrowing a catch phrase from my Dad, "Tomorrow's going to happen."

Since Mr. Basil didn't implode, that means Wednesday's HAND exam on adolescent lifestyles is definitely on.

"What if his forehead veins pop during the exam tomorrow?"

Borrowing a second catch phrase from my Dad, "One can only hope."

Karlos was nervous about the exam.

"Nothing to be worried about," I told him. "HAND teachers think they are actually teaching a real subject but they don't have a clue on how to even make a test. If you write your name on your test paper and stay alive and regurgitate all the crap he talks about in class, you're pretty much a HAND scholar. No worries."

Karlos looked at me as if he knew every word I was going to say because he did. We've talked about this during lunch and it's also the same exact speech he gives me before I take a math test except after you write your name on the test paper, you have to show your work and actually do the math and, if you're lucky, get the right answer.

Or close to it.

As long as you show your work.

Author's Note from the "Additional Irony" Category:
Basil is an herb that is very healthy for you in spite of its name. It has a good smell (It's part of the mint family!) and is also one of the key ingredients in pesto, a great green sauce. You should continue to eat pesto because it is delicious. If you haven't eaten it, try it.

Perpetual Adolescent Lifestyles

As I told Karlos, I'm not sure how you can study for an exam on adolescent lifestyles.

Sarah Tsippi could probably fail it, though. She thinks having perfectly color-coordinated binders and being a suck up with all her teachers, even Basil, means she can skip her adolescence and go right to college.

So she might even be cheating off of Karlos and I during the exam.

(Karlos and *me*... if you are reading this, Mr. Bloom.)

I guess, though, I might be considered the class expert since Basil singled me out last week. "Kro, you need a little more focus and elbow grease in class or else it looks like you're destined for a perpetual adolescent lifestyle."

Actually, that wouldn't be so bad.

As far as I know it.

So far.

Me. Poet/maybe.

Perpetual Adolescent Lifestyle

You know the drill:
pizzas
zits
hair starting to grow
somewhere
everywhere
body odor
screaming hormones
having friends
having more friends
betrayal by friends and family
losing friends and family
more zits
more hormones
voice changing
social pecking order
dealing with a too-tidy-who-insists-that-you-put-number-85-sun-block-on-even-
when-you're-staying-inside-the-house mother
being rejected or being the rejecter
doing
or
not doing homework
thinking about writing, kissing a girl for the first time or sports or all three while
simultaneously convincing my dad to take me and my invisible sister to live in
Moose Jaw, Saskatchewan, and living happily ever after there,
thinking about my first real kiss to a girl and not to Auntie Melba's furry
moustache, learning a Shakespearean sonnet to recite to my imaginary love,
doing dishes and chores
a huge new juicy zit on school picture day
slug teachers
slug kids
cultivating and harvesting more screaming hormones
(Yes!)
and, finally,
living in some kind of *fractal* (look it up!)-patterned family
unit
with chips and pickles, too.
And a shampoo-free front lawn.
Too.

—Kro Kandle

Basil, My Foot!

But, what Mr. Basil probably doesn't know and certainly not Sarah Tsippi is that I'm actually on to bigger things and ideas.

My own.

And Ernest's.

Since I'm already an expert on my adolescence, it's me who is going to skip the whole adolescent thing and go right into manhood.

Write a Book.

Ernest said.

So, I am. This is it. You're holding my first step to manhood in your hand.

And, you're reading it.

Really reading it!

I mean you're reading a book under the radar of your slug English teachers from hell!

That's cool.

Enjoy it while you can.

Enjoy it *if* you can.

Can you?

Just think—you will not have to answer any questions about plot, setting, characterization, theme, mood, symbolism, use of dialogue or anything asked by a diarrhea-of-the-mouth-driven Mrs. Pencey-type English teacher with a stomach that she tries to push in with her elastic waistband pants.

"Kro, I think you need to be clearer with your topic sentence," Mrs. Pencey would say. "What is your point, anyway?"

You just made my point, Mrs. Pencey.

I made it just like I wanted to.

The Wait

It's excruciating.

Months. Weeks. Days. Minutes. Seconds.

The Wait.

Worse than the wait before a math test is being passed out by the teacher.

Or before standing in front of a judge in *juvie* court. Okay, I really don't know about this from personal experience but I needed a powerful metaphor.

A good metaphor is great for descriptive writing.

The Wait has a two-edged sword because it peaks around the middle of August which also means that summer vacation is almost over, too.

"Kro, your eighth-grade schedule just came in the mail! Shall I open it?"

Even a slug parent has to know when to do the right thing.

"No, I'll come down and open it!"

"Well, the envelope does say – 'To the parents/guardians of Kro Kandle.' I'll open it and see—"

Jumping three steps at a time down the stairs was record breaking in and of itself. *Keep your eye on the prize,* I thought to myself, using the catch phrase of Mr. Florian, my non-slug PE teacher in elementary school.

I'm still thinking of what my catch phrase could be.

Still thinking.

My mom rarely brings me good news and this is one example of news that, at the beginning, is, actually, completely neutral.

But it will probably go bad at some point.

Like when I open the envelope.

Every summer you sweat it out.

What teachers do I have?

Are my friends in any of my classes?

Do I have to take HAND II?

When is lunch?

When is lunch?

Is there truth to the rumor that Mrs. Pencey moved from seventh grade to eighth and do I have her?

Would a note from my parents saying I'm sick of Mrs. Pencey and can't be in her class work?

There could be a whole chapter about her in my book.

Only thing is that kids would cry so much when reading about her that the pages would get so soggy and turn to pulp and no one would be able to finish the book.

And, besides, this book should be about my life even though Mrs. Pencey, whether I like it or not, at age thirteen, she is part of it.

Booger nasal drippings and all.

With a great spin move and a flying leap forward, I snatched the envelope from my mom's hand. She didn't even see it coming.

"I'll take that!" I yelled in what was probably the most bratty sounding voice I could muster. "It's my fate, after all."

My mom looked stunned. "It's not like you're going to be suffering in a dark, windowless, airless dungeon in eighth grade!" *A glimmer of humor, Mom. Nicely played.*

"I'll be the judge of that. There will probably be some windows," I smirked. "Anyway, it'll be pretty damn, um, er, *darn* close." Trying not to swear in front of my mom is like a dog trying not to salivate while dry food is being scooped into his bowl.

Pavlovian response.

Something I learned in English class and not in science! I try to learn to stay sane in science. It's my main goal!

How do I fit my life into a book?

Very carefully, as Mr. Bloom advised me.

Very carefully.

And it has to have the bad and the good.

The agony: My mom's too-tidy behavior, Mrs. Pencey, *the booger-nasal-infested-and-dripping, No One is Rushin' to Mr. Krushon's science class from Hades*, Mr. Basil's *HAND class from hell*, Mr. Dumplos's *butt-picking with his pencil during study hall* and the list goes on, having to neatly fold my underpants before I put them in my right-hand top dresser drawer as per my mom's rules and there are rules everywhere and anywhere whether you are looking or not.

The ecstasy: Knowing Ernest, writing my book, perfecting how to burp the alphabet as well as the "Happy Birthday" song, my best friends—Karlos and Campy, spending time with my dad, trying to figure out why I think about Campy so much—I'm pretty sure that's ecstasy and not agony.

I guess I'll have to make it all fit. This is my life and my book— ***running with slugs: the official handbook for living in a world surrounded by slugs.***

And slugs are everywhere.

You may even be one.

And you may even be dead.

And not know it.

Having a pulse doesn't mean a thing.

Many dead people have a pulse.

Your mother who thinks she knows what it's like to be an eighth-grade boy going straight into manhood has a pulse.

But she may be dead.

And doesn't know it.

She's too busy killing you. Metaphorically, of course.

Your ideas.

Your vision of leaping into manhood without a parachute or even an undershirt.

And making you wear deodorant.

Or not only making you fold your underwear but making you put your socks into tidy *sock balls* for your top right-hand dresser drawer.

Or for their drawer coffin.

Because everyone knows that the best underwear and socks to wear are picked right off the floor from under your bed.

Everyone knows that except for moms with sweaty palms who have the sense of humor of a flea and insist on being called *Mother* with a capital *M*.

I think there is going to be no shortage of things to write about in my book.

I'm keeping my eye on the prize, Ernest.

Author's Note: If reading about Mrs. Pencey makes you sob and the pages are getting soggy and pulpy, then possibly read this book on an electronic device but still try to avoid electrical shock.

Me. Poet/maybe.

Rapping Paper

My Family is all broke up into two
We were herded like animals in Noah's zoo.
It makes so I can't see the out for the in
And explain to you how hard that it's been
Can't meet her ex-pec-ta-tions to keep it clean,
Germfree—no way gonna be my kid scene—
'Cause I'm lyin' on dirty clothes on a bed never made.
Get off my back and stop trying to persuade—
ME that I am supposed to be made into you
News alert today CNN hot tip breakthrough.
Can't mold me like clay each year month day
More time with my dad is where my head wants to stay—
and my soul will float on a messy, sloppy bed
to cool Sas-katch-e-wan, jaw of a moosehead.
Where my poetry raps with beats of Canadian air—
and I will no longer be here and be happily okay there.

—TwoK

Me, Campanella Aminifu Mamoli.
Okay, Campy, for short(er).

Ernest who? Hemingway? Never heard of him until Kro kept talking about him day and night. Actually, I wouldn't know about the night part but I'm just guessing, and, I'm sure, Mr. Bloom, on some level, is sorry he introduced Kro to Ernest, as Kro refers to him mostly on a first-name basis.

It was Kro's latest new thing to get in totally obsess mode over! Although this time, really, this time it felt different and different for Kro says a lot.

He's different than most of the eighth graders at Hapworth. Eighth-grade boys, I should be clear to make my point, are a strange species, anyway. In Kro's case, given that he already has the weird eighth-grade boy chromosome gene going on, how many thirteen-year-old boys like sports and are pretty good at it, are funny and also write poetry as well as being obsessed with creating a new *non-slug world order* and reality for themselves like Kro is doing with this book.

Honestly some of the poetry isn't bad. Some of it is boy/grunt/complain poetry and he sees the world only in good vs. evil slugs and his other stuff is from the heart and asks probing questions and, sometimes, even has probing answers. I'm sure it's a bit of a stretch but stretch is good for an eighth-grade boy.

Writing poetry from the heart? Not caring what people think? Well, I think he really does care but he tries not to show it. The confidence thing he tries to project has a lot of dents in the armor, if you know what I mean, but Kro, I have to say, he does go for it. He really does and that really makes Kro different. Maybe unique or *sui generis*—I take Latin, too—because the boy does think and think hard about things and that, in eighth-grade *boydom,* makes Kro stand out because in eighth grade as a whole it is often boy*dumb*!

His book? This book? So very Kro. He's serious about this and taking Ernest—this first name business cracks me up—at his word.

Kro's going to do it. Somehow. I mean not just the writing the book part but the whole four things he's got to do for the "be a man according to Ernest" thing. He won't tell Karlos or me what the other three things are. I can only imagine. I really didn't even think he'd get the writing a book thing off the ground.

The two of us like to dis each other and talk some friendly trash. I even roasted him by suggesting what I think the other three things are that he needs to do to be a man:

1) make a two-egg omelet with one egg;
2) sit through a Mrs. Pencey English class without doodling his famous "Get me out of here!" cartoon characters depicted in a school jail;
3) tie his shoes without saying he is making bunny loops.

You get the drill. But it's cool. Kro will pull it off or stop talking about it or writing about it.

Or even cartooning about it.

Ernest or no Ernest.

Me, Campy/poetry from a quiet corner.

I see my reflection in the store window

I see my reflection in the store window
In black and white.
It's me.

Store mannequins behind the store window
don't look like real people.
I do.

My mom, Michele.
She's black.
One *l.*

My dad, Massimo.
Italian.
One *l.*

And they have me in common.
Although I hope I'm not that at all—
common.

I'm named for a baseball player.
Roy Campanella.
If you know about Jackie R.,
you might want to know about Roy—
and, then, a little something more about me.

I won't show you what I am writing or drawing.
You'll need to sneak a look—
But not toward that mannequin behind the store window.
That's not me.

~ C.A.M.

Me, Campy/poetry from a quiet corner.

Room to rent

There is room in the quiet corner of poetry

for

thoughts that play with crayon colors.

dreams with polka dot possibilities.

ideas on top of balloon bridges.

conversations in fantasy forests.

beliefs for days with runaway rain.

noise.

~ C.A.M.

Cool Campy

She's got *her* thing that is cool.
Very cool.
Without even thinking or knowing that she is cool.
How cool is that?

I'm not *there* yet.
The so-cool anti-cool not even knowing it's cool *cool*.
Cool.
Hard to pull off.
'Cause you're not aware of pulling anything off.
Or on.

But, we are alike.
When I say she's a lot like me, what I mean is that if she were a centimeter, I'd be an
inch.
Similar but different.
Or, if she were a foot, I'd be a meter.
This stuff might make good song lyrics, by the way.
And, if she were a pint, I'd be four *gills*.
Or, if I were one ounce, she'd be 437.5 grains.
(If my math is correct on all of these!)
But you get the drill.
A *commonality*.

She doesn't have any siblings unlike Karlos and me.
Not sure, at this point, anyway, if that is a good or bad thing.

Campy? She's a real poet.
Me? I'm working on trying to get there.
Got my poet name ready, though—TwoK—just need some good poems.

Most importantly, Campy hates PE but is actually more in shape and athletic than any
runner, baller or lacrosse player on any sports team at Hapworth. She runs the fastest 440 in the
school.
It's just that PE at Hapworth is, well, it sucks.
I know. PE is not supposed to suck in any school anywhere in the world but at Hapworth
it just does. I should know because I look forward to a class where you don't have to sit still in a
classroom and can actually move around and not get in trouble.

Bottom line: Sometimes you just want to see the PE teachers wearing real pants.
And think.
And blow a whistle at the same time.

Me, Campy/poetry from a quiet corner.

Are There Four Things to Do to Become a Woman?

Are there four things to do to become a woman?

Is it having one's own style?
And starting from being a young child.

Is it knowing it's not a race?
And I'll get there at my own pace.

Is it being happy at being thirteen?
And knowing where I've been.

Is it to enjoy the journey?
And my older self can show me.

There are four things to do to become a woman.

Start with being a thirteen-year-old girl.
And, be that girl.

~ C.A.M.

Math Heads Need Not Apply

I am not a math or science head.

I rolled the school dice or the school dice were rolled for me and I had one slug science teacher after another.

After another.

I never had a chance to have Ms. Ibraheem, the non-slug science teacher at Hapworth Middle School.

Don't think that math and science were my destiny, anyway.

And my destiny?

TBD.

To be determined.

To be *destined*.

I'm just following Ernest's plan.

See where that takes me.

The Moment

"Kro, what is the crux of what you are trying to say?"

I looked at Mr. Bloom and sputtered, "I don't know because I don't know what a *crux* is, Mr. Bloom." I sat there with a blank and I'm sure somewhat pathetic look on my face. I wasn't sure if it's cool or not to inform the class that you don't know what a word means or what is going on.

The class laughed but not the kind of laughter when a kid tries to purposely be a jerk or when the class starts howling because the rest of the class is thankful it's *you* on the hot seat and not one of them.

I learned that it's okay to say, in a way, "I don't know something."

And that was the anti-slug defining moment in my life.

Or, at least one of the major ones.

Even though it seems kind of small.

Small is big.

"Less is more," as Mr. Bloom would recite one of his catch phrases when talking about our writing.

There is something "more" out there.

There are ways to actively be an anti-slug.

I had to remember it so I'm writing it down here.

In my book.

Slug Philosophy in Words

"I mean, I'm trying to figure out if you can be alive and really be dead, you know, with your spirt and dreams."

Mr. Bloom looked at me with an equally blank look on his face but it was more of a *Can you give me more information?*

And, if truth be told, I didn't really ask him that question. I did in my mind but that is as far as it went. When I'm ready, I'll talk with Mr. Bloom about it.

Actually, Mr. Bloom was just waiting for me to say something.

Anything at all.

And, to the best that he could, he was trying to run interference for me as I stood there having a conversation in my mind but with nobody else.

"Kro," Mr. Bloom responded, "a crux is the main idea of something. The gist, the main idea, the brass ring, if you will."

"Oh," I said, and, weakly, "Thank you. I get what a crux is. It's not the past tense of crust, is it?"

A warm laughter wafted from the class and from Mr. Bloom, as well.

"Good save, Kro. Good save!"

It was.

What about the teachers that you have who stand in front of the class but are really dead. Their vital signs point to being alive.

I mean they probably even have a mouth full of spit—a sure sign of life!

And they can probably create even more.

Mr. Krushon's science class is all about life.

Except for him.

If you hold your pencil at an angle not acceptable to him—points off.

You have to exit his room single file if he has to take the class to a presentation in the auditorium during science class.

Hut-2-3-4, Hut-2-3-4, Hut-2-3-4, . . .

The military school of the mind.

And he even refers to HAND class as the Wellness Class.

Suddenly I don't feel so well.

And Mr. Krushon is always talking about the balance of nature. Well, rumor has it that he barbecues pork rinds on the heating vents in his room. That's about as close to nature as he gets.

The mantra in the hall: *I'm not rushin' to get to Krushon.*

Even with the lure of free barbecue.

It's the same with out of shape PE teachers. Again, not body shaming here. Being in shape can look and feel different for different people. I get that. It's just that Hapworth PE teachers don't seem to pay it much mind. As my dad says, "If you're going to talk the talk, you've got to walk the walk." I'm pretty sure he didn't make that one up but not sure where he got it.

So what is the slug philosophy of life that I have learned from them?

Do as I say, not as I do.

And, if a science class is about life, especially if it's life sciences, then have some life in it. If your science class has nothing living in it, including the *teacher, plants, animals*—okay, I know that furry animals are mostly not allowed in schools because of kids having allergies, and that is cool even though a kid might be in more danger from being bitten by Squeaky Andrews, the kid sitting next to them in the second-row science tables.

But a science class should have some living stuff in it, lots of living stuff in it, including the teacher.

Minimal requirement: one plant and some kind of animal, probably an *invertebrate* of some sort—except for ticks. Nasty!

Because isn't science about life, anyway?

It's like an English class without words.

Or a math class without a number or two.

Choose life over a dead science class.

With a dead science teacher.

Karlos Honah-Lee Webb
The Three Alliterations: The Third Member

Karlos knows death.
His dad, Howie, died last year.
That's tough on a kid.
Tough on the dad, too.

Karlos is a lot like me.
Except that he's not.
Which is good for both of us.
And everyone, really.

Karlos Honah-Lee Webb.
An interesting middle name.
Hyphenated.
Never saw one until I saw Karlos's middle name.
Haven't ever seen one since, either.

He does have an easy last name.
Webb.
It's got that whole Internet thing going on.
And, it's monosyllabic.
It just takes a hyphenated middle name to get to it!
Hyphens, if you're going to use them, at least put them in the last name(s).

You hear this middle name and you have to think, *Now, what kind of parent(s) does Karlos have?*
In my *weltanschauung* or world view, what really *is the slug quotient, if any or how much, that can be assigned to his parents?*

He's down to one parent.
Does that mean less complaining about the parent you have?
Or more complaining about the kid from the parent.
"Always look at all points of views when looking at a theme in literature," always cautioned Mr. Bloom.

When Howie died, my dad said, "Life has no script. No one knows the story line being written and you're in the middle of your own story."
Heavy, I know.
And you're in my story right now.
Don't forget.
You have a story, too.
And, I think, some free will, too.
Be in your own story.

"Kids are resilient," Mr. Bloom always says.
Have to be when living in a world surrounded by slugs and then your parent dies.
Imagine, then, dying in this world and it's surrounded by slugs.

It hurts.
Even if you have a *slug parent*.
Or two.
Has to hurt.
"Kids are resilient."
Has to hurt.
Mr. Bloom knows that, too.
He knows that you never forget that parent.
You just learn you have to learn how to live without that parent.
Most kids and people do.
My dad thinks that dead parent will always be with you.
Which makes it really suck that divorced parents hassle each other about being with their
kids.

Crap, it could be all over tomorrow.

With my luck, it would be after math or science class.

Make Number Four

Pre-algebra sucks.
Algebra, too.
No two ways about it.
Karlos is a math whiz so he doesn't get why I hate math.
Actually, I can do okay in math.
I just hate it.

The number four, however, is cool.
And, the number four—why?
Well, it seems that everything in life has a number.
- Going to the bathroom.
- Making a phone call.
- Looking at shooting stars (which aren't stars at all, by the way, but meteoroids).
- Playing sports.
- Counting things that you collect.
- Counting the number of *slug rules* you are supposed to obey.
- And, counting the number of parents, teachers, relatives or friends who happen to be a slug(s).
And those who aren't!
There really are some who aren't.
Sometimes they are in your own family.
Rarely.
Sometimes they are in your school.
Rarely.
Sometimes it is you.
Hopefully.

So, this book needed a number.
Karlos suggested the number *three*. "There are three strikes in baseball."
"Yeah, and then you're out," I countered.
"Babe Ruth's number was three."
"I'll give you that one. What else ya got?"
"Three-layer pizza is amazing!" Karlos always speaks from the stomach.
I didn't have a food comeback. "Four is better."
"In a championship run, 'Three-peat' sounds better than "Four-peat.""
"Four in a row is better. Doesn't matter how it sounds." I scored myself a math knockdown.
"You're not going to let go of *four*, are you?" Karlos demanded with a smirk,
"I won't forego it."
"Ouch!" His smirk was immediately accented by two arched brows floating over eyes looking to the heavens for help.

And, so *four* it is.
Starting with Ernest's *Four Things to Do to Be a Man.*

Four More

There are Four Directions—north, south, east and west.

One of them has to be the right direction for you to go when the *slugs* of your world are going to point you elsewhere.

Which is often and always.

Even a combination of directions is right because in life there is never just one direction that you can go.

Slugs don't tell you that because they are afraid to believe that.

They take one job in their life and will die in their jobs.

That's probably how your slug English teacher will end up.

Will anyone even notice?

You are a lifeless noun, Mrs. Pencey.

And not very proper.

Four eras of natural history—Precambrian, Paleozoic, Mesozoic and Cenozoic—so you can match each of your slug teachers' thought processes to the correct era of natural history that they belong in or probably live in.

- Four bases in baseball.
- Four downs in football.
- Four letters plus two in soccer.
- Four quarters in professional basketball.
- Four paws on Ambush, my golden retriever.
- Four Musketeers if you count D'Artagnon.

And four members in my family at my dad's house—my dad, my sister Chloe, Ambush and me, *TwoK.*

Not to be confused with *Tupac.*

He was an original.

Hopefully, I am, too, or on my way to.

Maybe I'll know more by the end of my book.

Venom of the Slugs

"Okay, like what is the antidote for living in a world surrounded by slugs?" Karlos asks me daily. I think he's trying to keep me on my toes or he just wants to bug me.

"Stayin' alive, man."

"Wow, deep. Okay—enough of the same crap, Kro," Karlos snaps back. He thinks my philosophy of slugs and their conscious aim to take over the world, since time began, is, for lack of a better phrase, *complete crap*.

"I mean really alive. You know, like Mr. Bloom says to live your life *with your antennae up*," I sputter as I try to continue.

"You're going *greeting card* philosophy crap on me again," counters Karlos, because he thinks he's got my number, which is four, by the way, and certainly likes to use the word crap a lot as do I.

I quickly counter and, okay, with a 'full of myself' attitude: "You know, live your life by seeing through the bullshit of teachers, parents, students and—"

"All teachers? All parents? All kids? Hey, do you see me standing here and talking to you, dude?" Karlos barks at me.

"Okay, oh wise one—the ones that are, you know, full of crap. The slugs of life!" My attitude suddenly gone.

"Geez, maybe you should write a book about it!"

"Thanks, jerk! Whadyathink I'm doing! It's a good thing I have a class to go to. *Death Science with Krushon.* Soon to be a major motion picture at a theater near you . . ."

"I'll buy the popcorn!"

"That'll be the day!"

Karlos is heading to math which he loves and I'm going to the guillotine of classes just hoping to come out of it alive.

Krushon is standing at the door as the students file in one by one.

"Do you have your science binder with you? If not, you will not be allowed to go to your locker and you will receive a zero for class preparedness for today."

Geez, will the planet survive?

"I have it, Mr. Krushon."

"And, class, once you're at your table, take out your homework. Today's assignment is on the board."

I tried to catch a whiff of barbecued pork rinds on his breath but I didn't want to get too downwind from him.

I might catch on fire.

During his class, I can't take the necessary time to figure out my life.

I have to concentrate on the life of an amoeba.

Can an amoeba recognize the venom of a slug?

Maybe, but it would probably have to be a very smart amoeba.

How does one recognize it?

It can be served in a Mrs. Pencey English class in a *pronoun stew.*

Or in math class sautéed with prime numbers.

In science class served on the periodic table.

Me, Karlos/Math Head.

"Kids need to know and remember their own history," repeated Mr. Bloom throughout seventh-grade English. I didn't pay much attention to it even though I heard Mr. Bloom say it a hundred times. I don't even think I knew exactly what he meant and then I knew.

I knew when my father died—to never forget.

Never forget.

He will always be there is what I think Mr. Bloom was trying to say but it is up to me to never forget. To never forget that. Right, Mr. Bloom?

My dad. What can I say? I have his memory, his impact and, this may sound weird, his smells. I can still smell the cologne on him, the cheapest knock-off cologne that was on sale at Target.

But having him dead, gone, sucks. "Kids are resilient," Mr. Bloom would say. One of our vocab words, too. "Work on your excellent memories." Okay, I will. Easier said when it's not happening to you.

Me, Karlos/Math Head/Numbers Poet.

Is there a number for death?

Dad?
Did you know that I was put in the highest math class?
Did you know that your guitar and amp are still in the basement?
Did you see that our Christmas cards went out?
Did you see your name on the card?
Did you celebrate with us?
Dad?

—Karlos Honah-Lee Webb

The "It" That Became Karlos

Karlos's house was a cool place to hang.

Howie was cool.
The anti-slug parent.
He was a first-name-only parent.
None of this: *How nice to meet you, Clarence. I'm Mr. Higginbotham, Reginald's father.*
Screw that.
I'm Howie, Karlos's dad.
Mi casa es su casa.
He always got that Spanish right!
There was always plenty to eat. Still is.
And, unlike my house, there was no *tía que lleva bragas de abuela*
swatting your hand because she was going for the bag of Doritos first.
As if it were the last bag of chips left on Earth.

Howie played guitar.
Always a plus.
And he taught Karlos.
Or Karlos learned by *osmosis.*
Okay, I learned something, Mr. Krushon.
But only because we had a test on it.

What a great thing to pass on to a kid.
Especially since Howie is no longer here.
Okay, physically, anyway.
Gotta keep that memory thing going.
And not pretend that what happened didn't.
It did.
And it sucks.
Bad stuff can happen.
No sense adding slug crap to life.
And slugs make a lot of crap.
Never take off your anti-slug antennae.
Ever.

What a legacy for Karlos—music and guitar: A way to meet girls, hang out, jam with
friends, dream of being in a band, having a passion in life and learning an instrument that is
easier to play on a beach or at a campfire than a trombone.

The basement was amp heaven.
A guitar museum.
The guitar museum has not changed even though Howie died.
No one is ready for that.
Not now and maybe never.

Not Karlos's little brother, Zip.
Annoying brother, BTW.
And not his mom.

Mom. *Mamá*
Marcella.
She's a *tejana.*
A Texan with Mexican roots.
She always reminds us of that and it isn't even a pain to hear.
Again.
And, again.

Marcella speaks Spanish and English.
As soon as you walk into their *casa*, it is a Spanish lesson, a *lección.*
Without the raw-egg farts of Mr. Krushon or butt-picking fingers of Mr. Dumplos.
She would repeat herself in Spanish each time she spoke to us.
Hi. *Hola.*
Would you like something to eat? *¿Quieres algo de comer?*

Howie's Spanish?
Well, his English was pretty good considering his family were cherry tree farmers in
Montana and they've been speaking English for as long as he can remember.
That's how Howie would put it.
His Spanish?
No lo habla bien.
He doesn't speak it well.

Okay, so how did the Honah-Lee thing happen?
What's the story?
¿Cuál es la historia?

Like a lot of stuff, if you know the story, it makes sense.
As much sense as anything can make sense.
Vivir en un mundo rodeado de babosas.
Living in a world surrounded . . . you know the drill.

The first name—*Karlos.* Good, solid name.
The name of Marcella's *papá,* Carlos.
Spelling Karlos with a *K*?
It was Howie's idea to pay homage to Kal-El, Superman's birth name on his home planet
of Krypton, before he was rocketed to Earth.

Okay, and here's the *pièce de résistance.*
Drum roll, please.
That hyphenated middle name—
Okay, sort of a long story.

Not too long . . . but a story, of sorts.

You probably can imagine or already know that Karlos, with having a middle name of *Honah-Lee*, has heard a lot of crap from the Slug Bullies that roam, graze and masticate all over themselves at Hapworth.

Okay, it does sound like a girl's name.

Worse things can happen in life. I know, Dad, but it's still a hassle for Karlos.

Especially on the first day of a class at the beginning of the year when a slug teacher reads the roll out loud for the first time and has to mention everyone's complete name with middle names and no nicknames, please.

Is that really necessary?

When the Slug Bullies hear Ms. Rheinhold, the anal math teacher, say in her whiny voice, "Okay, is there a Karlos Honah-Lee Webb here?" The Slug Bullies go nuts.

A pencil to the ribs of the slug sitting next to them.

Slug on a Stick.

Doesn't take much to entertain them.

Story, shorter:

Karlos' parents went to a concert.

A song that they liked, "Puff, the Magic Dragon," was being played. It has these lyrics: *Puff, the magic dragon, lived by the sea/And frolicked in the autumn mist/In a land called Honah Lee.*

The parents liked the lyrics.

The parents had a kid and said they would name their kid after that song.

The *it* turned out to be a boy.

The *it* became Karlos Honah-Lee Webb.

It's all good.

Hyphenated

Admission of fact as I see it:
a) It is a little weird to have a hyphenated middle name.
b) Honah-Lee does sound like a girl's name. Big deal, I know.
c) As far as hyphenated names go, it's not so bad. There are two kids at Hapworth with huge hyphenated last names: Daneshvar-McDermottroe or Chattopadhyay-Fenstermacher
Mouthfuls, both.

Sometimes kids with hyphenated names have former or current hippie parents even though I'm not sure that there are hippies still on Earth.
Karlos's parents are not former, current or wannabe hippie parents.
You could tell because if they were, their kid's first names would have been names like *Sky*, *Rain* or *Buckaroo*.
Or *Armistice*.

And, I'm not saying that former or current hippie parents always give their kids hyphenated names.
That's not a truism.
No facts to back it up.
Which makes it an opinion.

Karlos has survived pretty well with his middle name of Honah-Lee.
Are there more important things in life to worry about?
Not in middle school.
There are just other things.

Author's Note: Zip, Karlos's brother, is a nickname for Joaquín which is just a regular name. Further proof of no hippie parent bloodline.

Boy or Girl or

Another kid at Hapworth, Lee Galloway, has an interesting "name story" and it's also *Lee* related.

But with a twist.

Lee's parents chose the name "Lee" because it was gender neutral.
It could be a girl's name or a boy's name.
So, on a piece of paper, no one could tell if Lee Galloway was a boy or a girl.
Or undecided or still figuring it out or just *is*.

Interesting.
For two reasons:

It shows that Lee's—Lee is a guy, BTW—parents actually think about things and, I'm guessing, they might even be slug-free but, then again, I don't live with them.

And, secondly, it shows that they are cool because they are goofing on the perceptions of people who would see the name *Lee* Galloway as he was growing up and couldn't assume what gender he is.

Or isn't.
Or could be.
Or might be.
Very cool.
People would have to know Lee.
Completely cool.

Someone was thinking out of the box.
A thinking, interesting parent?
Oxymoron, perhaps?

Oh, Canada

Naming kids is definitely hard or maybe an art and, definitely, a way for a parent to make a statement about the world.

I get that.

And, it seems, when some parents run out of possibilities from baby name books or online searches, they look to geography—countries, continents and, even, territories.

One girl in my grade has the first name of Canada.

Two girls are named Asia.

One girl is named India.

Another is Montserrat.

Not sure why they are all girls with geography names although I have yet to meet a boy in my grade with the first name of Guam.

Real Pants

Johnny Kaczerowski is the best athlete at Hapworth M.S.

If he wanted to, he could pee in the middle of the gym floor in the middle of class and Coach Grady would say, "Good job, Johnny, good job! Now take that aim and that same kind of positive energy and use it for the game against Two Hills Middle School today after school."

Even though Coach Grady doesn't have any energy himself.

Especially for a PE teacher.

No energy at all whether it be positive, negative or electric.

He just stands there when he makes the team run laps around the field during football practice and looks disinterested.

Maybe there is something I don't know about Coach Grady.

Maybe he can leap tall buildings with a single bound like Superman.

And I just don't know about it.

Or maybe he really doesn't practice what he preaches which is, you know, *the ol' give 100% for the team thing!*

Someone needs to take his *slug temperature.*

It's not going to be me.

"What's a good way to remember what the theme of a book means? It's a literary device. Anyone?"

Mr. Bloom looked around the class. No one was biting but he had a few tricks that no matter how invisible and low energy everyone wanted to be that day, he could wake us up.

Or try to.

"Throw the football, Mr. B.!" called out Beechie Maloof, who tried to be too cool for school but really liked yelling out the right answers.

To impress himself.

The football came out from under Mr. Bloom's teaching desk that was in front of the room. It was one of those soft, plush "My First Football" footballs that you would get for a baby. It had to be soft so no one would get bonked in the head and not everyone could catch the ball when it was thrown to them, at first, anyway. He'd whip the football around the room looking for an answer.

For anything to light a fire in the class.

It would work.

Especially when Beechie took the bait.

"The theme is the author's message to the reader," he proudly shared. "

"Good work, Beech! And what's the mnemonic device to remember it?"

Beech looked a bit dumbfounded.

"You know, it's a memory trick to help you remember something," Campy whispered under her breath so she wouldn't show up Beechie. "You know, how do you know that a theme is a theme. Remember the 'th' hint . . ."

Almost screaming the answer, Beechie blurted out, "Because the *th* of *author* is in the word theme!" His smile could have lit up the ball that drops on Times Square each New Year's Eve.

And the entire Manhattan skyline!

"The *th*eme is the author's message. It's what the author wants the reader to know, to get from their book."

One of the themes of this book, I think, is about teachers who are the *do as I say, not as I do* type.

You know, art teachers who don't do art or English teachers who don't like to write.

HAND teachers who don't eat right.

And PE teachers and coaches who seem disinterested in being healthy and active while yelling at their teams and athletes to be healthy and active.

And, another theme: *Not all athletes are on the school sports teams.*

I don't think I'll ever be or feel disinterested in what I'm doing.

I love to eat, for example, and I'm interested in it but it's just too much work to eat at my house even though I do it.

My mom is too finicky about everything being in order and no one is funny at the kitchen table.

"Kro, pay attention! Did you put out a dessert fork instead of a salad fork?"

"Oops, I fork-ot."

Not even a smile from my mom.

I got one from my sister, Chloe.

But, first, she had to look over to see that Mom wasn't looking.

Progress, Chloe, progress. Keep going!

Some of my best comic material is wasted at my house.

I wish that when I was younger, I had an imaginary friend so I could reactivate him now. I am desperate for an audience.

Well, Chloe is starting to smile.

And tomorrow she might not.

There really is nothing funny about *cutlery.*

Perfectly lined-up cutlery.

Ready for the carving.

Of what?

Of whom?

Who?

Whose?

Please, Hapworth PE Teachers, wear real pants.

It'll get better.

I Got Zip

"Zip, if you mess with my school stuff one more time I'm going to smash everything in your room!" Karlos lashed out at his little brother. "How do you feel about reaching your next birthday?"

Good stuff, Karlos, I thought to myself. I try to stay out of family fights if I can. I can barely survive my own family fights.

"Oh, yeah, you and what army?" Zip screeched back.

Damn, that line is so cheesy, but somehow it works for Zip.

Zip could win an Oscar for the world's goofiest-looking kid. He has an almost sheep dog mop of long, black curls that came down to the top of his eyelids. It isn't clear if he could always see through the curtain of hair dancing on his eyebrows but it seemed he could always find or go after anything he wants.

Or destroy anything in his path.

And, when you're at a friend's house and your friend has an annoying little brother that his parent(s) think is wonderful, what are your options?

If any?

More Four: Salty

And as my dad would always say, "Everything in life is like the *four flavors* that a person can experience: sweet, bitter, sour or salty."

I could never figure out the last one.

What could he mean by an experience in life that would be salty—except if it makes you thirsty—so if you know, let me know, okay?

My dad likes to say things that make you *think,* really think, and you come back to him three weeks later after you think you have figured it out.

I thought the other three flavors worked pretty well to describe life's experiences. He would always say with a laugh when I asked him, "What does a salty life experience mean?" that having a saying that worked seventy-five percent of the time was still pretty good.

Meanwhile, I know what kind of experiences in life can be sweet, bitter or sour.

I'll leave salty up to you.

Unexpected. Create.

Always create the unexpected.
A key to survive in a world surrounded by slugs.
I'm not sure this is what my dad had in mind when he told me that quote but here's how I interpreted it and I'm sharing it with you.
It involves a chain reaction from my Auntie Melba and her oversized granny panties that she wears that are probably made from recycled all-season tires.

How to set up an unexpected and, at the same time, expected chain reaction from Auntie Melba:

1. Set up a giant slingshot.
2. Insert a strong, thick elastic as the springy element of the slingshot.
3. You will need more than one person here.
4. One person holds the tree limb that is the base of the slingshot.
5. The other person walks backward holding onto the pouch of the elastic which—don't put this in your imagination if you can't bear it—is made up of a pair of my Auntie Melba's oversized granny panties.
6. Insert a bowling ball (Black ball or speckled ball, only. No iridescent balls, please!) into the pantie pouch.
7. Pull back.
8. Release.
9. Most effective anti-terrorist *deterrent* ever invented.
10. Or imagined.

Me. Poet/maybe.

Don't Let

Don't let your family kill your spirit,
Even if it's far from a perfect fit.

You might have a mom who is way too formal,
Trying to make you way too normal.

You might want more time with your dad,
And the world's response is, "That's just too bad!"

It's a slug's life if you let them in,
And, then hard to remove from under your skin.

—Kro Kandle

Ironed Underwear

Caution: The slug warning signs in your family:

- If you have an aunt who irons her granny panties and her husband's *Batman* boxer shorts and wants you to iron your underwear.
- If your aunt's moustache is better than yours and she puts peroxide on her moustache to bleach it out.
- If you have an aunt that you wouldn't want to see naked—ever!
- If you have an aunt who hums marching band music all day long and sprays spit through the space between her two front teeth when she does.
- If you have an almost uncle who only asks, "Let's go to yard sales all day Saturday and look for old radios!"
- If you have an almost uncle who gives bad haircuts using an attachment from an old Hoover vacuum or his car vac.
- If you have an aunt and almost uncle who show up at your house unannounced and camp out for days.
- And days . . . .

Me. Poet/maybe.

I

I don't think

who I am is what you had in mind.

who I am is what you had in mind for a boy and a son.

                                    I don't think

who I am is what you had in mind for a boy who thinks.

who I am is what you had in mind for a boy/son who likes sports and writes

poetry

                                    I don't think

who I am is what you had in mind.

And

                                    I am here.

                                    —Kro Kandle

Free Time

There's a lot of free time in eighth grade.

At Hapworth, there is a *Quiet Reading Time/Independent Work Time.*

In my dad's day—he hates when I refer to it like that—it was called *Study Hall.*

I really started on my path to manhood and began to leave my adolescent life behind right there and then.

But, really, there's nothing else to do in *Quiet Reading Time/Independent Work Time* except count the number of times Mr. Dumplos cleans his ears with the eraser of his #2 pencil.

First the right.

Then the left.

And, then, yes, he puts it in his mouth.

I know it's gross but I had to tell you.

At least you don't have to touch the pencil like I do when he hands it to me when I sign out to go to the bathroom and I'm struck with frozen-in-ear-wax horror.

Could you imagine having to sign out to go to the bathroom in your own house?

Kro's mother said, "Now, will you be doing a #1 or #2? Kro, sign here on the magnetic pad on the refrigerator and it's the first door on the right. Don't forget to spray air freshener when you are done."

And you know what?

My mother would probably make me sign out to go to the bathroom if she really thought about it.

If she really thought about it.

I thank my lucky gecko stars that she really doesn't think too much about anything except being clean.

And, how to pretend that we are not home when Auntie Melba and almost Uncle Dewey just show up.

Gotta give my mom props for when we go into our *Auntie Melba and almost Uncle Dewey unannounced visitor lockdown alert* and we quickly pull down the shades and shut the curtains and crawl around the floor so we don't cast any shadows on the windows.

Sometimes it works but most of the time they just sit on the front porch and wait us out.

Auntie Melba brings out her TV celebrity crossword puzzle book and almost Uncle Dewey brings an old radio to work on and they both hang and get busy.

And we are trapped.

They know we have to come out for air at some time.

So *Quiet Reading Time/Independent Work Time* or, as I call it, *the Alcatraz of the Mind,* became my writer's studio.

I never thought that I would write a book but, as you see, I have to.

And I want to.

I have a lot to write—just to stay alive.

A lot to say.

About my soon-to-be-former adolescent life.

And probably yours.

We'll see.
But we'll start with mine.
And my leap into manhood.

Maybe this book will help you.
It will give you hope.
Or, at least, you'll stop dying—
mentally, *schooly*—in your family, and for you.
Hide this book from an auntie who wears oversized granny panties.
Hide this book from a parent who sucks the lifeblood
from you.
Hide this book from a Mrs. Pencey, the booger-nasal-infested-and-dripping, who insists
that you can only sum up the theme of a book in a one-word noun.
I have a one-word noun for her!
Hide this book from a slug-like parent who doesn't know anything about kids.
And doesn't even know it.

And show this book to those who you think can be saved.
Even those you think who can't.
You have to try as long as the elastic band of the *galactic underpants* still has some
spring in it and can hold everything in the galaxy together.
And we're all still here.
In one pair of very wrinkled *cosmic boxer shorts.*
And dirty mismatched socks.
Found under the bed of Saturn, of course.
Even with the slug in the moon waiting for you with its Cheshire grin.
All you have to do is try.
And try some more.
And never stop even when you overhear your mother talking to her aunt about who owes
whom five dollars from when they went shopping together.
And, they send a bill to each other.

So, just never iron anything.
Flossing is good.
Just don't put used floss in your pocket.
It's really okay if you do.

And always check your pulse. Your pulse of *living.*
Not just your pulse of *life.*

So, I dedicate this book to Ernest Hemingway.
To the number four.
To my dad.
To, okay, my mother who is learning how to deal with Auntie Melba and almost Uncle
Dewey and showing some anti-slug progress. Baby steps.
Some, BTW.

To my invisible sister.
To my dog Ambush.
To the night sky when the street lamp is out in front of my house.
To a basement guitar and amp.
To my first real kiss with a female who doesn't have a moustache and isn't related to me.

Update:
Mr. Dumplos has four ear picks with his grading pencil so far this period!
A new record for one period.
Keep it up, Mr. D.—just don't correct any papers with that pencil.
Or touch anything at all in the school!

Next

"Ernest, what do I do now?"

"Plant a tree."

"What the . . .? Now I have to do gardening?"

Part Two
of
the
Four Chambers
of
the
Heart

—The Right Atrium—

"Plant a Tree"

Never confuse movement with action.

—Ernest Hemingway

Metaphor

Plant a tree?
I don't get it.
I mean the writing the book part; that's hard work. It really is a challenge. Somehow, I'm going to come out a different person on the other end.
Or, at least, a person who has written a book and, according to you, Ernest, that's a good thing.
An important thing.

But there's got to be more with the *plant a tree* thing.
That's what I think, anyway.
I mean, I can just go in the backyard of my mom's house or find some scrawny space near my dad's house and plant a tree.

It can't be that easy.
It's a metaphor, right?

Right?
Okay, then for what?
And, so what?
You said it yourself. *Never confuse movement with action.*

I'm ready for action.
I want action.
Okay, I need action.

Me, Karlos/Math Head/Numbers Poet.

What are the odds?

One in four challenges in process, dude—
Keep going, doing good.
But will this be enough?
Now the going gets really tough.

This is something you have to finish—
Becoming a four-steps man is your wish.
I give you credit for sticking with it—
That Ernest must really know his shit.

For me, it's pretty easy.
Just surviving the booger-nasal-infested-and-dripping Pencey.
Can you always play the slug upper hand?
Then no one can catch the gingerbread man.

Your goal is different from me, Kro—
You're like a modern-day Thoreau.
Take the road less traveled, my friend.
Catch your breath every now and then.

Try and not overthink all this stuff,
Even when the going seems pretty rough.

—Karlos H-L Webb

Plant a Tree

It's not getting me psyched like Ernest's write a book challenge.
Maybe you could already tell.
Okay, I don't get it.
Sounds pretty lame.
Ernest, what were you thinking?
I want to be a man, not a gardener.

There's something fishy about it.
Something not right.
Something just too simple about it.
Maybe that's it, I don't know.
I know I don't know enough.
Yet.

Am I stuck at the write a book stage with nothing to show but a book at the end and no manhood?

Plant a tree.
Big deal.
Don't get me wrong.
I like trees.
You know, the whole tire swing from a tree thing.
I like the shade part, too.
Climbing. Cool.
I know the whole producing oxygen and removing carbon dioxide and contaminants from the air part. Okay, just so you know, I got that from my own reading, not from Mr. Krushon.
Bird habitats, can't forget bird habitats, especially for crows. I have a thing about crows.

Established: Trees are important.
I get it.
I don't get it in regards to Ernest, though.

Plant a tree.
These words feel like an opened, half-full box of your favorite off-the-*MyPlate*-nutrition-chart-presweetened-candy-breakfast-cereal that's been left on the kitchen counter too long.
Stale.
 It was good eatin' in the beginning but the box was left open and the contents got stale.
Stale.

And, sometimes, I've learned from writing this book, upon Ernest's request, is that words can get stale if there is nothing behind them and I'm definitely not sure what's Ernest second challenge is for me.
I want to be a writer and an adventurer.
Not an Ernest-mini.

But a Kro-man, if you will.
Kro-Magnon man.

I've got nothing here.
Nothing = the absence of something.
An indefinite pronoun even though it refers to something.
Only nothing.
It's action that counts. That's what I'm getting from him.

Ernest was a man of action.
Planting a tree.
Auntie Melba is not a person of action.
Neither is almost Uncle Dewey.
Although I have to admit he did find some cool old radios even if he couldn't get most of them to work.

I can talk about writing a book but that doesn't mean anything unless I do it. So if I plant a tree, you do the math. Where does it get me? In about twenty or thirty years, maybe a tire swing, some shade, something to climb, oxygen to breathe, less carbon dioxide and contaminants and more crows.
All good stuff.
And the skills needed to plant a tree.
A square shovel? Maybe more?
But is it worth the wait?
Ernest, you're killing me with this one.
Where's the action?

The only action from a tree, as I can figure it, is if one falls on you on the way to school. That could be a plus, however, if you don't have your homework that day. Other than that, not a whole lot of action except for the falling leaves deal but that won't happen for a few years, at least.

Facta non verba.
Deeds not words.
Thank you, Ms. Kazakh.
I'm actually using one of the Latin phrases you taught us.
And, much to my surprise, I have to say.

I'm still trying to figure this *plant a tree* thing out and it's not coming to me—easy.
What are you trying to tell me, Ernest?
When people talk, listen completely. Most people never listen.

Okay.
But what am I listening for?

Me, Campy/poetry from a quiet corner.

It was that afternoon

When you said everything had to change—
The colors of fall were getting brighter.
Oranges, browns, gold.
But that wasn't enough for you.

Changes around you were not changes within you—
The colors of an autumn rainbow did not matter.
Inside you there was a season that had no name.
Because you think the answer is found outside of you.

Is that how change happens?

~ C.A.M.

Get the Message

Until I can figure the *plant a tree* thing, I'm sticking with the writing the book thing.

I have to stay on track with that, stay focused.

Maybe, and, hopefully, it'll come to me as I write this book. One thing I know for almost sure is that it's a metaphor I'm looking for although how do you look for a metaphor?

Online search: *Metaphor. Metaphor meanings.*

Advanced online search: *Metaphor meanings that can change one's life and propel one into manhood as inspired by writer and adventurer Ernest Hemingway.*

Not really getting any good results that I can use.

So far.

Anyway.

Ernest wasn't known to hit his readers over the head with a message. His writing was very direct and, as Mr. Bloom would say, "untangled."

I've got to untangle this myself and go and find it.

Who has time when my almost Uncle Dewey chases me around my mom's house with Hoover vacuum extensions yelling, "You need a haircut! You need a haircut!"

No, I don't. I need a metaphor.

That I get.

TKAM. Ruined.

Speaking of metaphors, have you ever had a terrible teacher?

If you say no, you're lying.

I mean, not just a bad teacher, but terrible.

Life-threateningly bad.

The kind that might keep you from getting up in the morning and doing your best fake groaning theatrical interpretation of "I'm not feeling well this morning. Can I stay home from school?"

And, here's the metaphor as to how terrible a teacher I'm talking about: As if a tuba fell from the sky and landed on your head on your way to school kind of terrible.

Note the metaphor. (Would this actually be a simile, BTW?)

I can write them.

Just can't find them too well.

At this point, anyway.

If not, and you want that experience, meet Mrs. Pencey, a *quantity not quality* type teacher who has the brains of a barn door.

An open barn door!

She even ruined the assigned reading of *To Kill a Mockingbird*.

That's a hard book to ruin for a class.

I mean, how can you assign TKAM and not even get into the background of the case of the Scottsboro Boys?

Good thing my dad filled me in.

I can't even imagine if Scout ever had a teacher like Pencey what kinds of psychological warfare they would have had.

Pencey the booger-nasal-infested gives a TKAM assignment and these were the only questions from the class:

How many pages do we have to write, Mrs. Pencey?

How many pages do you require, Mrs. Pencey?

Can we handwrite it in blood—red, blue or black, Mrs. Pencey?

Why are you teaching, Mrs. Pencey?

What are you teaching, Mrs. Pencey?

Did you have any friends growing up, Mrs. Pencey?

Do you have any friends now, Mrs. Pencey?

Do you like yourself, Mrs. Pencey?

Do you?

You.

I know you're hoping you can read this book without thinking too much. You just want to get through the book and say, "*Hey, I read a book. I'm an amazing person!*"

And, maybe leave the thinking to me.

Then, you can write the assigned book report, tell a parent or two of yours, your teachers, and don't forget the librarian at your school—who will probably flip—that you read a book and then they all think you're some kind of reading wonder and an amazing kid.

If you're homeschooled, don't worry. I'm sure there are plenty of people around you that you can tell.

Just walk outside. Look both ways, first, so you don't get hit by a bus, truck or a taxi rickshaw.

Then tell the guy who runs the dry cleaner or sub shop on the corner.

Even a cop directing traffic or a guy operating an excavator.

Or the farmer down the road.

But, really—just don't *tell* anybody you read a book.

Have an *opinion* about it.

You probably do have an opinion about most things anyway.

Like what time you should come in on a Friday night.

Or should your shirt cover your belly button.

Or is there a God or should there be homework on weekends?

So, why not have an opinion about a book? I mean you put in all that time to read the thing, you might as well keep on going with it. You can usually do an opinion in one sentence so it really is not that much more to do.

That is, it doesn't require a whole lot of *thinking*.

At least the thinking that is required in school—*Puke Thinking*!

The ol' *PT*!

PT will definitely get you through school but there could be more to life.

I think.

Or so I'm told.

Or want to believe.

I think Ernest would agree with this: I want to go beyond *PT* even though the adult world, and much of the kid world, is not ready for it.

You might not even be.

And a lot of the time I'm not because I'm still trying to figure everything out even though I'm being taught in school not to.

I'm really thinking and just trying to stay alive.

Really alive as I watch Mr. Dumplos decompose before my very eyes and choke on his ear boogers while he chews on the tip of his pencil eraser.

A graphite slug snack!

Sit Up

Sit up (straight) for a second while you read this next sentence: *You* might be dead and not even know it.

Checking your pulse will not help. *Having bodily fluids is not proof of life either.*

Dead people can have pulses.

And fluids.

Really, they can.

Mr. Dumplos died during third period last week on a Wednesday and he still doesn't know it.

So did my science teacher, Mr. Krushon. He got terrible indigestion after snarfing down a giant beaker of Diet Coke and then gashed his head on a solar system mobile hanging by weakened red threads from the fluorescent light in the ceiling.

He has an indentation of a papier-mâché Jupiter over his right eyebrow.

And he still thinks he is alive.

I would tell him that he isn't but he wouldn't listen to me.

Would he?

Being *school brain dead—**SBD**—*is a socially transmitted disease that you are not taught about in school and, specifically, in HAND class because you are too busy making *MyPlate*-nutrition-for-teens posters because your body, as Mr. Basil says, is growing in so many different ways and needs food from each of the five food groups.

Anyway, the *MyPlate* nutrition guidelines will probably change sometime soon so there might be new material available for a new poster.

The poster assignments from HAND classes around the world cannot be stopped and they are the most serious environmental danger in the world today that no one in the government or even in the news dares to talk about. They are the driving force behind the leveling of rain forests, old-growth forests, trees on city streets and in suburban backyards, even, to keep up with the demands of poster board for HAND posters about *MyPlate* nutrition for teens?

Being **SBD** is the worst kind of death because, usually and quite unfortunately, you aren't aware of your own *demise*.

Demise—a *vocab word* from seventh-grade English. Again, thanks, Mr. Bloom! I knew I would use that word sooner or later.

Either in my book or in a poem.

But never in my own book.

So, with *demise* I write about *life*.

Deep.

I know.

WARNING! Reading beyond this point in the book is not for the faint at heart! It requires *gut-thinking - GT*! Maybe for the first time. Thinking with your gut. And, with your brain. It's kind of like a value-combo meal of thinking. Really thinking.

Back to Basics

Before I totally *succumb to my adolescent urges,* as Mr. Basil says, *gut-thinking* is basic.
Or should be.

It's the kind of thinking that is connected to your brain. That may sound like an *abstract concept* and a bit hairy because it scares grown-ups half to death!

Especially slug teachers!

And kids, too.

Especially slug kids!

You get the point and it's not a stupid one, I don't think.

Because I want to think.

As much as people don't want me to.

I want to use my brain before I unconsciously sip more slug venom and breathe in more slug air as the **slug teachers of the universe** are slithering and squirming to get into my—and your—ear canals, eyeball sockets and nostril cavities and try to capture my brain and squeeze the membranes or amoebas out of it or whatever is left.

So, take this warning.

You.

Caution: *Adults, especially, and certain dead teachers, don't want you to do any gut-thinking.*

I guess you can call this a **Living in a World Surrounded by Slugs Rule:** *Don't let an adult catch you really thinking about something—especially on a school assignment or in response to a question. They can't handle it. They just can't.*

And won't.

Gut-thinking will get you in trouble.
But, it's worth the risk to stay alive.
Choose life.

Gut-Thinking

Plant a tree.

I got nothing.

Me. Poet/maybe.

How do I love to gut-think?

How do I love to Gut-Think? Let me count the ways.
I love to Gut-Think to the depth and breadth and height
My soul can reach, when feeling out of my slug teachers' sight
For the ends of being and the anti-slug race.
I love to think to the level of every day's
Most quiet need, by sun and Batman night-light.
I love to think freely, as young men stuff their appetite.
I love to think purely, as slugs wait I disobey.
I love thinking with the passion put to use
In Hapworth Middle, no slugs need apply I sayeth.
I love to think with a power I received from Zeus
and reading Mark Twain. I love thinking with the breath,
smiles, tears, of all my life; and, if Ernest choose,
I shall but think better every day. How many ways can I
Gut-Think?

—Kro Kandle
    and with glacier mountains of apologies and thanks to
    Elizabeth Barrett Browning and her Sonnet 43.

A Great Grey Slug

Of course, a teacher will always ask you what YOU think about something.

The teacher means it about as much as he or she looks forward to coming back to school at the end of summer and then boring kids to mass *bore-icide* from hearing stories about the new deck Mr. Andrews, the tech teacher, built with his brother-in-law while wearing sleeveless white undershirts dripping with sweat and jam stains from donuts.

Who can save me from this image?

In case you forgot, back to what to do when a teacher asks what YOU think about something.

And if you really tell him or her, you're screwed.

Big time!

They want the kind of thinking that's not connected to your brain.

What they want is what adult wolves do for their pups when they return from the hunt. The pups lick the faces of the wolves to stimulate the regurgitation (puke!) impulse so the adult wolves throw up the food for their young.

Chow time!

Come and get it?

Get what?

Get it?

The adults only want what they think you *should* be thinking.

After all, they have a curriculum to follow.

Sometimes a curricu*dumb*.

Sometimes a curriculum that will put the teacher on the *same page* the same exact day each and every year.

Time doesn't pass by calendar pages.

But by curriculum pages.

Any real thinking will make Mr. Dumplos poke his pencil right through his head via his ears!

Could anything really stop it, anyway?

They especially can't handle it if your answer, or question, brings up the real truths of the world.

Like, should ketchup be refrigerated or not?

Or is bombing a village of innocent people wrong?

Trust me on this.

Better yet, try it out.

Just be ready to duck.

Adults say one thing and mean another.

So do kids.

It's a skill learned early on.

An early survival skill of *Living in a World Surrounded by Slugs.*

So, welcome to *my* world, by the way, and all of its slimy *inhabitants.*

Great social studies word, by the way—*inhabitants*! (Even though you put me to sleep, Mr. Rhine, most of the time last year, I do remember *that* word. It's too bad because I *love* social studies but hated *how you taught*! I mean, c'mon – the big term paper for seventh grade was *evaluated* by *how many note cards you take and turn in*?)

Puhleeze!

File Mr. Rhine in the *slug category.*

Big time.

A Great Grey Slug!

Not to be confused with the *Pointed Slug.*

Because, rarely, he rarely gets the point.

Redundant, I know.

Mr. Bloom would have a cow.

No one will tell you the truth but they will ask you to always tell the truth.

And they will always tell you how many note cards are required to do so.

Be careful out there.

And don't say I didn't warn you.

For the **four** stages—maybe—of schooling.

It's elementary,

middle,

high school and

college (if you want to or need to).

Period.

Then life.

Not really if you are already dead.

Life fluids or not.

BTW.

It's your life.

Not theirs.

Deer in Headlights

This is what you need to produce for *gut-thinking, GT,* for short:

A one-sentence show-off/deer-in-headlights opinion that really shows that you're not dead from the eyebrows up.

But, if you show you are not dead—**look out!**

This is how you do it: Drop an opinion and then start leaving to go somewhere—fast—to avoid a follow-up question which will be designed to *tear down* what you say because you're a kid.

Because you're a student.

Because you aren't dead like your teachers—yet—if you can help it.

They won't be happy until you are *dead* in your thinking.

Because kids aren't really supposed to think.

Unless it's what an adult thinks.

Or can be corrected by an adult.

Or shown in index cards copied word for word from the Internet.

There's always an adult follow-up question because he or she will have an opinion on your opinion.

Which is cool.

Unless it's an "That's an interesting thought, but . . ." (Hey, they usually forget to say the 'interesting' part.)

Just to put down your opinion.

And then they offer their own follow-up before you can offer your counter opinion: "You're too young to understand that—"

Or—

"Yes, but what if—"

And while you're ready to stand your ground they have already followed up their follow-up with another follow-up.

And you follow up by becoming *The Obedient Listener*: TOL.

Because you had an original idea.

And probably a good one, too.

And it goes on.

And on.

Studies have shown that adults have more opinions on kids' opinions than there are numbers in pi.

And their opinions turn into speeches.

And you're the audience.

Of one.

As your body fluids begin to dry up.

Quickly.

And immediately.

What do you do when you have an attack of GT—gut-thinking?
Practice this:
Drop and leave.
Eventually you can work up to: Drop and run.
That's the advanced course, however.
Here's the bottom line: Always leave them wondering.

Here's a sample opinion to try out.
It's not an example of GT so there won't be any repercussions.

Here it is: New and improved/color and bleach safe.
This opinion can be used mostly on all books and it will effectively dodge or prevent any adult comeback to beat you down.
Trust me.
Here it is: "Oh, I like the way this author (me, by the way, in this case) uses short, crisp sentences almost like writing *a combination of the elements of poetry and prose*." Not bad.
Food for thought.
The adult is mulling their next move to counter your opening move.
I'll even throw in some reasoning why I do it just to make it easier for you in case your getaway is blocked by a pole, another adult or quicksand or the *eternal slug air* of the universe.
Here it goes: *It's my writing style to combine a sense of the beat and rhythm of prose and poetry. I like how it looks, how it reads and how it sounds. It fuels the pulse of my writing.* (High-minded sounding of me, I know ....)
And, it's my book.
Period.
Me.
Not anybody else. My story to tell.
And no adult can get into my head.
Or a dad or dads or a mom or moms.
Not even a gap-toothed auntie who saves all of her used floss in case she ever runs out or an almost uncle with burned-out radio tubes stuffed in his front pocket that rip every red plaid flannel shirt he's ever had.

No one can offer an opinion to change *my* story.
Not even if you're also a kid on the verge of an adolescent breakthrough.
Or on the verge of manhood.
Like me.

Maybe this book will help you be you. I hope it does. It's already helping me. I think.

Here's another good opinion to throw out to someone—this book is written in the genre of a coming-of-age story.
You know, teen rebellion, self-awareness, sadness turns into joy, truth and hope and happiness and the American way and that kind of stuff.
Realistic fiction. Except it's not.
It's my life.

POV

Teachers will probably call this book a coming-of-age story and dissect the hell out of it until you or even I wouldn't recognize it anymore.

Wipe your booger-nasal-infested-and-drippings, Mrs. Pencey, and get ready to see how many ways you can ruin the experience of reading this book for every kid you "teach"!

They talk about truths in a coming-of-age book.

The POV—point of view—is of the narrator's telling their story of the struggles and triumphs of the young teen protagonist—a fancy word for the main character in a story. By the way, I'm also the protagonist in this story so I hope that helps your report and I am the narrator, too. So this story is told by my point of view—first person. Now is that cool or what? You've covered the genre, who the protagonist is and what the POV is. Your book report is going to be great but keep reading as the protagonist gropes with the challenges of growing up and self-discovery.

In a world surrounded by slugs it's a challenge.

One more thing: The point of view I am using is *first person limited*. I can only write about what I know. I can't get into the head of the other characters as much as I would like and know what they are thinking whether it be my parents, Chloe or my dog, Ambush.

I can't pretend what Campy or Karlos are thinking even though I know them pretty well. They can only speak for themselves and that is what they do in my book.

Often, I think I know what is going on in Mrs. Pencey's or Mr. Dumplos's head, for example, but that is only pure guesswork.

Pure speculation, as Mr. Bloom would say.

But I do have a lot of evidence to back up what I think they are thinking.

Yeah, never can know for sure.

People are complex. Thanks for that one, dad. Not very helpful for my book, though, as I presume to know all that there is to know about my slug-inhabited world and its inhabitants.

And, more.

Just look at your teacher right now. If your teacher is cleaning out their ear with a pencil just know that earwax sticks pretty well to a pencil. It could end up on one of your papers.

And get into your bloodstream.

When your teacher gets up from their chair, see if they pick their pants out of the crack of their butt and just think where their hands have been when they pass out papers to the class.

I know, what an image!

That's another point for your book report: A good writer uses wonderful descriptive language in order to create images for their reader and that's what I'm doing for you. I hope so, anyway. So, in your book report, make a note that the language is rich with description once again and that vivid images have been created for you, dear reader!

And if they have a glazed look on their faces, they're probably *slug dead* anyway.

Frozen in a time.

Then sit back and try to picture your teacher when he or she was your age.

I know it's hard.

It's hardest to do for the *slug teachers* that you have.

Because it takes imagination to picture them as students once or even young and they don't want you to have or use imagination.

Although their imagination died so much earlier.

And earlier.

They just want to get yours.

All of your imagination.

Block them with a blitz of *anti-slug venom*!

Which is this: You will **always** have your imagination.

They can never get it from you.

You will always have your imagination.

And your own experiences.

And your own observations of things.

Always.

I got those three things from a writer named William Faulkner.

Okay, I got it from Mr. Bloom who got it from William.

Now you have it. *Imagination, experiences, observations.*

Always.

Thank you, William.

Me, Campy/poetry from a quiet corner.

I was there when

I was there when
you had imagination
each day with the noonday sun.

I was there when
you had your own experiences
and hard times you needed to express.

I was there when
you had your own observations of things
as you always went for the brass ring.

I was there when
I asked you if you believe everything that you write
or do you just hope that one day everything will be all right?

~ C.A.M.

Note Cards

And what is *anti-slug venom* that will help you survive in school?
The magic ingredient?
Note cards.
Just use note cards.
And more note cards.
And still more note cards.
Fill out zillions of note cards for your research paper, for example, and hand them in and they'll sit happily at your teachers' desks.
Your note cards.
Which required no thinking.
For either of you.
Just as long as you filled out enough of them.
So that it counts.
Number them.
And it will *really* count.
Not for you.
It never will.
It just counts.
For your teacher.
For your slug teacher.
Who will have an engraved granite note card on their grave instead of a tombstone.

Got pencil, Mr. Dumplos?

Me. Poet/maybe.

The Big One

The shortest answer is doing the thing,
Ernest said.

Not when it comes to note cards,
Kro said.

Making note cards bites the big one,
Kro continued.

—K

Note to Reader

Dear Reader,

Please remember that I am writing this book for my own purposes on my quest to manhood and while I'm very glad that you are here—because books are written to be read—this book is also being written for my own rite of passage. But, I really am glad that you are here, really, I am. Okay, don't throw up from my sickening display of sincerity. I can barely stand it myself. But, as Ernest helped me structure my life, maybe I can help you and if that seems too lofty a goal, maybe you will just enjoy what you read and/or get an easy book report out of this.

I'll try to help you in any way that I can but you know the drill—you've got to help yourself first which I think is why you are reading this.

A book can help change a life—writing or reading one—just don't tell your English teacher. They'll ask you to write a report on why or how 'it' changed your life and how it happened to you.

And, you know, you can't write an essay on what happens in your soul.

How come only you and I know that?

School systems have not yet developed statewide tests on how to measure your soul. Yet.

Only you can do that.

Please don't die too many deaths in English class or any other class. Stay alive at all costs! It's important for your *life*! Your teacher will try to kill you with memorizing the entire list of prepositions and also tell you to do a plot analysis from backward to forward until your brain gets fried and, of course, you end up hating the book and even hate reading which is really the sick thing because reading could be a one-way ticket out of *Slugsville*.

They're just into *dissection*.
Dissecting a book, a story.
Dissecting your soul.
Your life.
Your ideas.
And then setting up a lit circle or book group so you can discuss a dead book with a small group of classmates—who haven't read it.
Don't plan on reading it.
Will never read it.
And probably won't be able to find their copy of the book, anyway!

So, take your soul out for ice cream or listen to some music.
Just protect it.
You will have taken a first step against *slugualism*.
Congratulations.
I'll never tell.
But you will be able to feel the difference—immediately.

And, look out for metaphors.

Sincerely yours,

TwoK
(aka Kro Kandle)

Me, Campy.

This being Kro's book, it can be hard to get a word in edgewise. It's probably better that he gets out all of his philosophy on paper on the peril of the existence of human slugs in the world. I mean, really, he does have a point. Have you ever been in an English class and tried to have a discussion on an assigned class novel and hardly anyone has read the book? Sometimes I'm not even sure if the teacher has read it.

It's good, though, to have weird friends or should I say *interesting* friends. Kro and Karlos both fit into that category without a doubt.

Do I think it's obnoxious that Kro refers to Mrs. Pencey as the booger-nasal-infested-and-dripping-one? Not sure if he is using this as a metaphor or what. Don't you think that is something a thirteen-year-old boy would say? Would a girl write something like that?

In this instance, I can't wait for Kro to grow up to be a man according to his "friend" Ernest. Sometimes he can be a bit too graphic and descriptive as in over the top. Okay, he can be that way a lot of the time. It is, though, what makes Kro, Kro. Gotta love him!

I think it might be lost on Kro and Karlos, too, that Mrs. Pencey is a human being.
"Prove it!" is Kro's usual response.
"Where's the data?" Karlos always chimes in. He's a math and science head.
Here's the eternal question: Why do boys find booger references funny? Kro was trying to be sophisticated by adding in *nasal-infested*. Girls don't think booger references are necessarily funny or clever. Why is that? Superior species is my only guess! ☺
Don't get me wrong, though, when the guys talk about Pencey that way, she might deserve all the junk she gets. It's just how they do it shows how more mature we are than boys. This is probably not news to girls who are reading this.
Did you catch any of this, Kro? ☺
Did you catch your metaphor, yet?

Me, Campy/poetry from a quiet corner.

Did you catch a metaphor today?

Was the spring flower garden a bed of luminescent jewels?

Were the butterflies a day sky of winking sparkling stars?

Was the child a conductor of the wind orchestra quartet?

Were the birds the trusted messengers from one tree to another?

Was the winding country road a grey ribbon leading to a castle in the woods?

Were the forest's leaves an audience applauding the breeze?

Was the truth a river that flowed over smooth and craggy rocks?

~ C.A.M.

Basic Freedom

When my Auntie Melba comes over with one of her unannounced visits from New Hampshire, there are many unnatural land mines to be avoided.

Tripping over oversized granny panties lying on the floor could result in serious injury.

Not to the underwear.

It's made of aluminum.

Which makes me want to add one more phrase to the *four* basic freedoms outlined in a speech by President Franklin Roosevelt on January 6, 1941 (Did I mention that I like to read—anything and everything—including cereal boxes and small appliance warranties?):

1) Freedom of speech and expression

2) Freedom of religion

3) Freedom from want

4) Freedom from fear *and your family* (at least those family members you want to escape from with your soul intact!) and their oversized underwear left drying in the bathroom on the shower-curtain rod because they have to be hand-washed and air-dried.

The words in italics I added are mine, not Franklin's.

I just didn't think that Franklin went far enough.

Breath, Spit and Fart

Vampire slug parents (VSP) control every **breath**, **spit** and **fart** of their kids!

Do yours?

My mom tries to do that to my sister and me.

Have to admit, though, she's improving a bit because so much energy is spent with fending off Auntie Melba and almost Uncle Dewey. *Thank the anti-slug god for them!* (Did I really write that?)

My mom has earned her *VSP card,* believe me. In her case, she was born with it as I am sure it was not passed down from her parents.

Because everyone says, as I already wrote, that my grandparents were so cool—all four of them which is an algebraic anomaly (look it up!) bordering on worthy of consideration in the Guinness World Records book.

It just proves how very slug-like the universe can be in that I didn't get to know them.

What happened to the gene pool, then?

Random.

It must be from Auntie Melba who has the worst bat breath.

I guess that's what happens when you try to swallow hair, eyeballs, bones, and raw human emotions from your closest relatives—me, Chloe and my mom.

Hard to admit we are all of the same flesh and blood.

I guess my mom is just trying to survive her family, too.

Wait—was that *empathy* on my part?

Good thing Auntie Melba and almost Uncle Dewey never had children.

The bad thing is that she thinks the three of us are her children.

Almost Uncle Dewey is just along for the ride.

Almost Uncle Dewey talks about his old radios with more affection than he talks about us.

And Auntie Melba is always looking at department store catalogues so she can buy her favorite oversized granny panties on sale.

"The oversized panties are more comfortable that way," Auntie Melba would share. Why she is sharing that information with me is anyone's guess.

Or maybe she should look at boat catalogues and search for *sails* and combine a *mainsail* and *jib* so she can sew her own oversized granny panties.

Without her getting seasick.

Or anyone else.

Not very cool to write about, I know. I get it.

Still thirteen and *growing and changing* as Mr. Basil would say . . .

But, really, just solidly thirteen in most ways.

Endure

The twelve labors of Hercules were nothing compared to what I have had to endure in eighth-grade English from hell.

In other words, being asked to capture the bull that was ravaging Crete or to steal some golden apples from Hesperides' garden is nothing compared to having to write Mrs. Pencey's famous killer essay assignment on regurgitating literary devices used in *To Kill a Mockingbird*.

Auntie Melba

My mom insists on being called "Mother" with a capital *M*.
She's very formal.
I know, how did she get me for a kid?
She must've gotten all that slug-stuff from Auntie Melba who insists on the "Auntie"
part.

My mom is just not funny.
Can't tell a joke.
Doesn't know a good joke.
Can't even take a joke.
And the worst thing of all is this—she doesn't even have a belly laugh!
None, nada, jamais, zero, zilch—dinosaur goose egg!

Auntie Melba is not funny, either.
When she visits, which is often and for a long time, there is no laughter.
And if you look ever so closely you will see that slugs cannot laugh.
They physically can't do it.
They don't have the power.
Or the will.
Or the willpower to laugh.
Especially at themselves.

The house my mom grew up in was always about quiet.
Even though the grandparents were cool.
I guess they thought that quiet was cool.
Even when there was yelling, it was always about quiet.
That kind of creepy-quiet like in a scary movie.

Auntie Melba rarely laughs because she is always eating.
Our food.
Nonstop.
And if she isn't eating, she's thinking about eating.
Or dreaming about it.
And, it's always our food.
Even in her dreams!

Just don't go to a restaurant with her.
We'd go to a fast-food restaurant or some kind of regular old restaurant and she'd want to
be treated like she was the Queen of England or at least the Burger Queen:
"Young man, how much salt do you use in your cooking?"
"Oh, Miss, does this dish contain any fats?"
"If I eat the tablecloth or napkins, can you tell me how many calories that is?"
She has just made eating her occupation.
It is her job.

It was either discussion about her weight during dinner or how to lose weight once the dinner was over.

And, she is always on my sister and me to eat right.

My mom cooks pretty good and she buys healthy stuff.

Which I eat except for the chips that I sneak.

And, the Doritos.

The chips and Doritos are my contraband.

My little sister, Chloe, weighs as much as a flea.

She burns enough energy and fat to light a kerosene lamp every fifteen minutes.

If people still used kerosene lamps.

"Here, Chloe, eat some pie," Auntie Melba would say as she shoved a plate of pie under Chloe's chin.

And, when Chloe wouldn't eat it because she doesn't like sweet desserts, which Auntie Melba knows, she would snatch the plate right back and snarf the pie right down in seconds flat.

Probably earning a Guinness World Record in the process.

Auntie Melba has one speed: slow and irritatingly slow.

Okay, that's two but you get the point.

Except for eating.

The only exercise she has is shopping.

For food, that is, for her *own* house *and* for her oversized granny panties.

Which is okay because I've always felt that if I were on a boat way out to sea with my family and the ship's engine died and we were about to sink, I could use my Auntie Melba's oversized granny panties as a sail and we would safely sail back to port.

And, if our home were ever attacked, that underwear would make a hell of a slingshot!

If I'm ever about to drown or my family is under attack by an invading terrorist army, please let my Auntie Melba be nearby.

That's one good thing about relatives who visit and never leave: A certain sense of safety and security from a terrorist attack.

Author's Note:

If Auntie Melba and almost Uncle Dewey don't leave the house soon from this recent visit, Dad, can you please take Chloe and me and move to Moose Jaw, Saskatchewan?

Or, just me.

Around to Write

Ernest did not mention that the four things that I must do to be a man would tend to get more difficult as I got more into it. As you know, I am writing this book on his expert advice.

That's not to say that writing a book is easy.

It's not, trust me.

I mean if you think *reading* a book and *liking it* is hard, try writing one.

But, I have to admit.

I like writing this.

And I like writing what I wrote.

You should, too.

I mean like what you write.

Are writing.

Have written.

Why not?

If you have to read a book in the first place for school, then this book could be it. The book is the whole truth, as I know it, with no additives, preservatives, trans fats or teacher edit marks (in red, blue or purple pen or pencil) added.

And, once you finish reading this book, and you will, please be reminded that I have completed my first step—giant step number one—in becoming a man in "my world according to Ernest."

Maybe it can be part of you becoming a man.

Or a woman.

Or a person.

Or any or all of the above.

These rules can be for anyone.

And everyone. Even you.

When I first read Ernest's list of four things to be a man, I thought there might be an easy way around all of them. You learn these life skills of how to get around things in middle school, especially at Hapworth where the school mascot is, or should be, *The Bellyfoot Slugs.*

Great name for a band, though—*The Bellyfoot Slugs*—live in concert!

I learned that Hemingway actually wrote the shortest novel ever.

This gave me hope.

And still does.

The novel was six words: *For sale: baby shoes, never worn.*

It is said that Hemingway called this his best work.

It is pretty cool and says a lot.

I don't think a six-word book or six-word memoir would count for my 'write a book' challenge to be a man.

Even Odysseus couldn't figure out a way to get around that one!

Which makes me think what is it about this *plant a tree* that has me stumped?

Pun, intended.

Hero Non-Worship

Ernest is not my hero.
Nobody is except my dad and, maybe, just maybe, me, one day.
In a weird way I look up to my grandparents who I didn't even know.

I mean how can a famous person be your hero if you don't even *know* that person?
Because if you choose a person who is well known for doing or being something to be your hero, you're going to discover that that person is, well, just really a person.
With good stuff and bad stuff.
And, maybe, a lot of good stuff and a little bad stuff.
Or the other way around.

My dad says that people are complex. People are not black and white.
Even Gandhi. I bet he would have gotten really upset if one of his robes wasn't washed properly and folded the right way. I also think that there are probably people in India who think that he didn't go about his business the right way.

Or Mother Theresa. I'm sure there were times when she couldn't find one of her sandals and she went ballistic.
Or, Mother Theresa's version of going ballistic.

And, while that person may have done something pretty cool or new or exciting in sports or technology or in the movies or in music or in life, he or she is *still* a person and can also do some stuff that is not pretty cool or new or exciting especially to one's kids like—

- being cranky all of the time
- picking their teeth in a restaurant
- texting while driving
- acting like a slug-bully with your kid's teachers or coaches
- being a jerk in day-to-day life while making gazillions in high tech
- getting chosen the Super Bowl MVP and being violent to women off the field
- making fun of an aunt's oversized granny panties

Heroes in sports and music are marketed like corn flakes and dish detergent, deodorant or acne cream.
Do you want your hero to be whole-grained, biodegradable, smell nice and not have zits?
And, while all of the ingredients will be listed on the box of that hero in the media, in real life all of the ingredients are not.
Admire what someone *does* or *has done* with their life but don't make that person a *hero*.

You can write about that person in a six-word book with the info that you have.
Or about yourself in your own *six-word memoir* like Mr. Bloom had us do.

Me. Kro.
My Thirteen Six-Word Memoirs
If only they could count as a full book . . .

Caution: A pencil dipped in earwax.

Ernest made me do it. Thanks.

I'm homeschooled. No slugs here. Not!

Beware: Principals with hairy, thick arms!

A slug vampire parent lives here.

Karlos knows numbers better than most.

Campy knows hearts better than most.

Write a book. Plant tree. More.

My school is surrounded with slugs.

Kiss a girl; no moustache—hers.

Oxymoron: Survive English class with Pencey

Four challenges to be a man.

And I will do it, man.

Me. Campy.
Fourteen Six-Word Memoirs

Soft. My poetry is not loud.

See me through the store window?

Karlos will get over the pain.

Black and white. Everything all right?

Karlos will never forget his dad.

Annoying brother/Like Zip. Want puppy.

Poetry is there. Does anybody care?

Roy Campanella: Get to know him.

Kro will tackle the four challenges.

Read my poetry today. It's open.

Harper Lee did write another book.

Do you believe what you see?

Do you believe what you hear?

I don't need more than fourteen.

Me, Karlos.
One Dozen Six-Word Memoirs

I talk to you every day, Dad.

Zip. Will trade for a longboard.

Numbers. Numbers × numbers = numbers.

Sueño. Each night. *Mamá* cries. Sad.

Kro is cool. And weird. Original.

The Three Alliterations: Do duck down!

Is Kro right about slug theory?

Trying my hand at poetry, too.

Question: When will it stop hurting?

Saw Kro moustache hair. I think.

Hapworth math = easy 4 me.

Rage against the dying/good night.

Plant Face Hair

I wish Ernest had said *grow a beard* instead of *plant a tree*.

Not that I could or anything but I could *say* I was growing a beard. It's just that it's in the germinating stage. It's getting ready to grow. Who knows?

It could start in a day or two.

A month.

Maybe a year or two.

But it is starting.

Eventually.

I mean it will.

Won't it? I'll ask Mr. Krushon to develop a secret formula.

My beard being *planted* is not enough, I guess.

And, as long as I'm going after the *Four Things to Do to Be a Man*, I probably shouldn't screw it up with a lie.

Plant a tree.

Trick question, methinks.

Too easy.

I have to try harder.

Nickname

Did Ernest have a nickname?
Yes, he had several.
I researched it.
And, no, I didn't make a PowerPoint presentation of it.
I can barely stand doing one for school.
I'm not going to do one on my time!

His sister, Sunny, called him Oinbones.
Some other nicknames were:
- Champ
- Ernestoic
- Tatie
- Wax Puppy
- Bumby
- Wemedge
- Ernie, Hem or Hemmy.
- The most famous one of them all—Papa.

Every nickname has a story.
Mine? I didn't have one till fifth grade.
My dad and I sat down and we decided that the time was right for me to have one. My real name? Ezekiel. Zeke, is what I liked to be called. That can be considered a nickname but it's really a shortened version of my full name. I was after a bona-fide-unattached-and-unrelated-to-my-real-name nickname.
And that's what my dad and I set out to do.
Okay, and I wanted the nickname to be an alliteration with my last name, Kandle.
Very important.

Me. Poet/maybe.

Got Wings?

A crow can fly.
It circles the world from way up high.

A crow has wings—
Cut loose from a mother's apron strings

I will get wings—
And listen as my voice sings.

A slug can only slither—
Any wings have been left to wither.

This Kro can fly.
Live your life is the battle cry!

Me—TwoK.
Slugs—get outta the way!

—TwoK

Plant a Nickname

Could my nickname connect me more with Ernest?

Some were family nicknames. Some other people gave him.
Some he gave to himself.
Just like I did although I only gave myself one.
But, then again, I'm not a man like Ernest.
Not until the end of this book, anyway.

My nickname, as you know, is Kro.
It was just time to have one so I gave myself one—with help from my dad to get the right
metaphor.
Can't get away from the whole metaphor thing.

No need to wait for someone to give you a nickname.
DIY—Do It Yourself.

Do you have a nickname?
If not, get one by the end of this book.
It can't hurt.
It won't hurt.
It can only help.

Circle U.

When you have to fill out your information for state standardized testing you fill in your proper birth name.

Your nickname you can keep for yourself.

You've heard a teacher follow the script they have to say when giving directions on how to fill out your personal information in your answer booklet—with a #2 pencil, of course:

> If your answer booklet does not have a Student ID Label on the upper right-hand corner, you will carefully, thoughtfully and with great determination and intent print out the letters of your last name in the space provided in the Student Name Grid.
>
> If your name has a hyphen, it doesn't on this form. Write your hyphenated last name together as one word.
>
> After Last Name you will see a dividing line.
> Print your First Name here.
>
> Print your middle initial in the last box under MI.
> If you don't have a middle initial, why not?
> Or get one.
> Under the Student Name Grid, you will see a box of circles.
> Fill in the circles under each letter that you printed under the Student Name Grid.
>
> When you are filling in the circles, it is important to completely fill in the circles and to fill them in darkly which will also be a reflection on how much you have learned and were able to retain from when you were first taking school directions and learning coloring in kindergarten to now because any stray marks outside of the circle will not be read or understood and we will know at that moment that the slug education system where you live has failed you.
>
> And, in fact, because we can't trust you, this form that we need with your name and ID number will forever now be done for you electronically and we will determine what name(s) to use for you.
>
> And no more bubbling in your name and information in the little circles will be necessary. That was the only fun part.
> No longer.
>
> In fact, you will now take the whole test electronically and on computers.
> You can now use your #2 pencil to poke your eye out because you have to take this test.

High-Steaks Testing

A twist on high-stakes standardized testing:

Wouldn't it be great if the meat-eating students in the world would receive a gift of a T-bone steak dinner after taking their state's annual high-stakes standardized tests?

That's it—you take the test and get a steak.

Taking the tests would be much easier to digest.

For vegetarians and vegans?

A tofu pupu platter, perhaps?

And for the pescatarians?

A salmon dish or canned tuna, perhaps?

For the flexitarians who can justify eating meat, chicken, seafood or going veggie whenever they want?

No prizes for you.

The High-Stakes Testing System wouldn't know what to do with you.

Sorry.

You'd have to first commit one way or another on the proper "Official Food Preferences" form three months in advance and stick to it.

No bubbling necessary.

Teacher Nicknames

This can be hazardous to your health.

Especially if you blurt it out by mistake.

Ms. DuFarge, my math teacher from below hell and somewhere between the Earth's inner and outer core, has a name that is too easy for nicknaming.

Dangerous.

I am not a math freak in any way and, as I've said, I don't like math. Too many damn numbers.

And I don't like math games like sudoku, math bingo or Math Scrabble.

But, if a math game can ease the piercing pain of math, I'm all for it.

Anyway, Ms. DuFarge wouldn't do a fun math game with the class even if her hair were on fire but that's beside the point.

Her name—DuFarge. It's almost too easy to make an evil teacher nickname out of it: DuFarge = *DoFart*.

Or, for the more literate student, a quick *DoYouFart?*

The worst is if a teacher's evil and somewhat clever nickname slips out in class with a brilliant question like this, "Excuse me, Ms. DoYouFart, can you go over the order of operations for this problem again?"

But, probably, you won't even be able to finish your question because either you'll be so shocked and probably be passed out on the floor and writhing in pain or in anticipation of pain from having let the *Ms. DoYouFart?* slip out while the rest of the class is also in silent stun stage or hilariously laughing which just makes it worse for you.

There's no way out for this self-inflicted wound on this uneven Earth.

By the way, Ms. DuFarge, is the world monomial or binomial?

Malta

Are there slug teachers in Malta? Probably.
Slug teachers who speak Maltese.

They are probably on the nearby island of Gozo, too.
Not sure if they speak Maltese there.

Slugs are everywhere.

BTW: Don't worry if you don't know where Malta is or have never heard of it. You can look it up on the Internet in five seconds. Just know that *slug education* knows no boundaries. That's the important part.

Author's Note: *A self-chosen nickname can help to cement and ward off your non-slug identity with a slug teacher. Even in Malta.*

Plant a Fart

Just wanted to write that and see it in print.

And, Ernest, why couldn't you have put this on your list?

Easy one.

Guidance: Meet Your School Counselor

Do you have a guidance counselor or school counselor in your school?
If you don't have a good one, no matter what you call it, you're still screwed.
No metaphor there.

They have to have an answer for everything because they see almost everything come through their office that can possibly happen on Planet Earth or, in this case, Planet Hapworth, a much weirder place.

Each and every single day, from the tons of students, some very weird, some not so much, and some just eighth-grade typical, who report to them.

And some of the kids have legitimate (great word!) things to talk about or work through. And many don't.

If I were a guidance counselor and for the kids who kept bugging me about the stupid stuff all day, I would just say, "All I can really do is try and change your schedule," to try and shut them up. I think it would work for many situations, but not all.

"Ms. O'Reilly, a five-hundred-pound gorilla just escaped from the zoo and has taken over the seventh-grade lunch period!"
All I can really do is try and change the gorilla's schedule.

"Mr. El-Sayed, the sun just fell out of the sky and my science room is on fire!"
Let's talk about a room change.

"Mx. Watkins, this morning my bus ran into a truck transporting uranium and I think I'm radioactive."
I do have an old Geiger counter around here somewhere.

"Ms. de Miquel, *the wheels on the bus go round and round all through the town and the wipers on the bus go swish, swish, swish* and I start to hum and feel the urge to sing."
All I can really do is try and change my schedule in case you return.

Drama

It's an epidemic in middle school.
One foot in the front door of the school = drama.

And the guidance office looks like a Greyhound Bus waiting room with kids who didn't do their homework or don't have their projects that are due or who have drama.

That's the real drama—kids just want to get out of class or get a piece from the candy dish on the school counselor's desk.
Kids just don't want to be where they are supposed to be.
Can't say as I blame them when the slug-teacher ratio to non-slug-teacher ratio is off the charts high in the slug-teacher favor!

But, really, it's mostly a con by the kids.
Kids love conning school counselors.
They get to miss a class, a test or not have to hand in a long-term project because they are in the protected, sacred and hallowed halls of guidance.

Some students always have *drama*:

Zari didn't say hello to me in the hall!—Catalina

I left my hat on the bus and it wasn't even my hat. It was my brother's.—Mehmet

I'm feeling sad that Mr. Sanjoy is teaching transitive verbs. I hate transitive verbs. I don't know what a transitive verb is. Transitive verbs scare me.—Aleksi

They ran out of chicken patties in the lunchroom. I'm stressed and need to talk.—Darsh

What is another name for thesaurus?—Hoi-Ming

I've been eating pencils. Is this okay? Am I weird? Should I switch to pens?—Carrick

Everyone in my family is right-handed but me. What does that say about me?— Miyu

Ms. Stans says "crap" in math class all of the time. What would happen to me if I used the word crap in class? Why do I have to put up with that crap?—TJ

Own It, If You Can

If you are lucky to have a non-slug school counselor at your school like Ms. Chen, visit regularly and often.
It could be your haven.
In a school surrounded by slugs.
But you will have to look hard—

If you screwed up, Ms. Chen's response: *Own it*.
Short.
And sweet.
Then she would go from there.
No crap could be passed on her.
She couldn't be conned.
She saw through the *drama*.
Kids would even stop their drama between each other before getting to her office.
Because they knew they weren't going to get anywhere with it.
Students knew it.
Ms. Chen knew it.

And she'd be there for you.
And with you.
No candy dishes.
No waiting lines of kids trying to ditch a class or get out of taking a test that they didn't study for or have their homework or project done.

And because kids knew they couldn't get *over* with Ms. Chen, they were out of luck.
Or, in luck.
Because they were Ms. Chen's student.
A student of Ms. Chen's.
Cool.

Me, Karlos/Math Head/Numbers Poet.

I went in to talk

The words were not coming out.
The words had no place to go.
My mom said to talk to somebody at school.

                              So I did.

The line to the guidance office was two before me.
Usual suspects of kids trying to cut class.
I was trying something, too, trying to talk.

                         If I could.

It was my turn and I didn't want it.
I'd be in class if my dad were here.
I walked into his office and started to talk.
"Excuse me, Karlos, I have to take this call from Principal Hardy."

                    I stopped talking.

                              —Karlos Honah-Lee Webb, a son

The Cool Crowd

Life gets more complex in the halls of middle and, probably, high school. I'm just guessing but how could it not?

Just look at the drama in the halls of your school with the *self-proclaimed popular, cool, loud and look at-us crowd because some of us might have physically matured faster than you and we are going to show off our bodies while we still have them as we eat our way off the new food plate or inverted food pyramid requirements or whatever the latest government geometric-shaped food categories are into junk food heaven so we probably have a year or two at most looking like this until we blimp out.*

One more time, no body shaming intended.
They are shaming their own bodies.
And probably yours.

How to stop or, at least, tame the cool crowd?
Offer them a fried Twinkie.

Author's Note Regarding Twinkies: If the manufacturer stops making them or stores stop carrying them or they are just too hard to find, anything doughy and fried or sticky will work.

Me. Poet/maybe.

Hair, today

B   e   y   o   u.

Dye it

Style it

/c/o/m/b/i/t/

C
 U
   R
 L
   I
T

Straighten it_____

Iron it.

Grow   *d*   *r*   *e*   *d*   *s.*

Shave it.

Or just
       wash
       and
       dry.

Change it.

Or not.

Do something and stand for it.

It's not permanent.

It's always growing.

S   o   a   r   e   y   o   u.

—KROKANDLE

Life questions to ask yourself on the way to school

1. Should clean socks be rolled into little, tidy sock balls?

2. Why is the school boiler always breaking down in February?

3. Should ketchup be refrigerated?

4. Who voted on your school's cool and popular kids to be the cool and popular kids?

   a) What does it mean to be a cool and popular kid?
   b) Who cares?
   c) Why does this self-identified group care so much?
   d) Is this cool world their whole life and reason for being?
   e) Do they peak in life as an eighth-grader?
   f) Who really cares?

5. Is Jupiter's surface really made up of liquid hydrogen? (A brown-nose question just to please Mr. Krushon.)

6. Where do I fit in a world surrounded by slugs?

7. How do I fit in a world surrounded by slugs?

8. Should parents be required and licensed to have a sense of humor?

9. Do hissing Madagascar cockroaches make good classroom pets?

10. Should pineapple be allowed as a pizza topping?

Me, Karlos/Math Head/Numbers Poet.

Odd/Even

Wind.
What is it?
It's moving air.

The Earth's surface is heated unevenly.
Unevenly.

Life works unevenly.
Families do, too.
So does life.

Uneven.
Odd.

—Karlos H-L Webb

Be careful what you volunteer for

Ernest learned firsthand about the *uneven Earth*.

Right after high school he took a newspaper job with the Kansas City Star. He left the newspaper job after six months and went with his buddy, Ted Brumback, to become a Red Cross ambulance driver in Italy during World War I.

As it turned out, lots of would-be-famous-writers did that, too, in their search for adventure.

Ernest wanted to join the army. His dad didn't want him to.

Ernest, as you can probably guess, was headstrong.

He did try to enlist in the army but he was rejected. He had poor vision and failed the eye exam.

Even Ernest failed tests.

And was able to make the best of it.

As a volunteer in the Red Cross Ambulance Corps, Ernest did see plenty of action and a lot of it wasn't pretty. When there was an explosion near an ammunition factory, it was Ernest's job to pick up the human remains.

That couldn't have been fun.

Ernest was injured when he was working as an ambulance driver. He was hit by a mortar shell and it left shrapnel in his leg.

He was also hit by machine-gun fire.

And he showed bravery on the battlefield by dragging a wounded Italian soldier to safety.

He received the Silver Medal of Military Valor for this.

Which I guess is kind of like being on the school honor roll.

Okay, a lot more than that but if you're a kid, you take what you can get.

Ernest gained cool experiences at great peril to himself.

Adventures and experiences that fueled his later writing.

Write what you know.

He was a tough-guy writer on an uneven Earth.

Scientific Investigation

I suffered through Mr. Krushon's teaching about the steps of the **Scientific Investigation** process. It's his version, anyway, so I don't even know if it is accurate.

I do know it was torture.

But I turned it around for me. I use the rules of a *Scientific Investigation* as a way to recognize and snuff out the slugs in life.

- **Problem:** Figure out what the problem is. Ask questions. For example, were there always slugs? Or, what happened to the gaggle of slugasaurus that lived 65 million years ago and whose fossilized remains were recently discovered on a rocky beach of the Wakamow River in Moose Jaw, Saskatchewan?

- **Observation:** If you can, get to that rocky beach on the Wakamow River and do some archeological digging. If you can't, go online and do some virtual digging.

- **Hypothesis:** Here is where you take the facts you've gathered so far and see if you can explain away the *demise* of the slugasaurus *enclave* of the Wakamow River and how it was rebirthed or morphed into human teacher or parent form. *Hypothesis #1* and the only possible hypothesis that I can come up with is this: There is no explanation. Slugs pop up everywhere, in all shapes and forms, in all extinct and current animal and human species, in all families, in all genders and in all genres of literature and, even, in beautiful places like the shores of the Wakamow River in Moose Jaw, Saskatchewan, as well as down the hall from your bedroom or in front of your English class or next to you in math or at your bus stop and, without a doubt, in the daily slug hell—the lunch line.

- **Experiment:** In the *Experiment* step of the *Scientific Investigation*, I'm supposed to come up with some kind of a test under controlled conditions that can see if my hypothesis is *valid* or makes sense. Well, since my hypothesis is that *there is no explanation* for the existence of slugs, we can skip this step. It can't be traced to water or air supply because we all share it and, sometimes in a family, one kid is a typical kid and the other might be a slug but they both drank the same breast milk or formula so slugs just form. Maybe they didn't have a plan to grow up like Ernest's four-step plan to be a man.

- **Conclusion:** This is where it all comes together. I've examined my data from my experiment and now I can draw a conclusion and the conclusion is: *I feel like doing a PowerPoint on the existence of slugs.*

That should tell it all.

Okay, Plant a Tree

I'm trying to apply the scientific investigation method to my plant a tree problem. It has gone from challenge to problem in a pretty short time.

And, that's where I'm at—at the 'problem' stage and trying to figure out what my problem is.

Plant a tree.
Seems pretty clear cut.
Pun intended.
It could make as much sense as a talking metamorphic rock.
Sometimes simple things are not as simple as they appear.

I'm still stuck on this metaphor thing.
Scientific investigation or no scientific investigation.
Seems pretty straightforward, though.
Can I make it into a metaphor?
Why not?
Worse things have happened in life.

Is it a simile?
No *like* or *as* is in it.

Which of the four kinds of sentences is it?
Probably imperative: *A sentence that gives advice or instructions or that expresses a request or command.*

As you probably know and I probably know that you know because if you are reading my book, you probably have more brainpower than bacteria, exceedingly more than an arthropod and absolutely more brainpower than gravity—not much going on there. *Force that pulls objects toward each other.* We're not talking jab step, crossover or rocket step b-ball moves here.
Pretty straightforward.

Ernest is being pretty direct.
I don't think he is messing around.
Getting to manhood only happens once in a person's life.
If you miss it, I think you're out of luck.
Not sure what a plan B would be.

Just so you know, I also had my own personal list of things I had to accomplish before I got into this whole *manhood* thing. In my case, it was a list of *Four Things to Do in Order to Be an Official Kid.*
To be an *OK = Official Kid.*
OK?

And the envelope, please:
1. To learn how to *fake burp*.
2. To learn how to *fake burp* the alphabet and have a conversation in *fake burp* or to speak conversational *Burpese*.
3. To learn how to open my eyes *underwater*.
4. To understand what the *Federal Reserve Bank* is and does.

1. Fake Burping:

First, I learned how to swallow the proper amount of air in order to make a short, fake burp. I then learned to do staccato burps—very short bursts of air with sound. Then, with practice, I extended the *short fake burp form* to an elongated sound in 4/4 time.

2. Fake Burping the ABCs and Conversational *Burpese*:

My first goal with fake burping the alphabet was an obvious one. I tried with the *A* sound and then continued on down hitting all of the letters and, really, was cruising all the way from A to Z, my *Alpha and Omega*. I was even able to do a guttural version of the ABC song.

No small feat.

Having a conversation in *Burpese* is not as easy as it may appear.

First, you need to be fluent in *Burpese*, yourself. Second, in *Burpese*, you need to find a person who is fluent or equally as fluent as you. Somehow, you find each other. For me, it was Karlos. He's very good at *Burpese*.

One of the best.

3. Opening My Eyes Underwater:

The anticipation of opening your eyes underwater is actually worse than the real thing. I was conditioned, as most of us were, to think that bare eye and water didn't mix. And, that's what I did.

I developed my plan in early elementary school.

One day, when Karlos and I walked to Cumberland Pool, I put my plan in full motion. While we were walking, I'd look for the best *diving stones*. An excellent one should be slightly bigger than a quarter, dark in color and flat.

We'd sneak them into the pool and throw them in. Of course, Karlos and I were competitive as to who could retrieve the stone first. I'd use the foot method and try to find the stone with my foot—at first.

Karlos was eyes-wide-open in the water and would not only get the stone first but he would make a point to tap my big toe with the stone once he retrieved it.

The competition of the diving stones and the purpose of it forced me to open my eyes underwater. I tried cautiously at first by standing in the water and putting my head level with the water's surface, much like a crocodile or hippopotamus does.

Slowly and ever so carefully, I'd sink a bit lower and see how long I could keep my eyes open as the water rushed in, and felt like my eye sockets were filling with vinegar.

Squinting to see halfway above and below the water horizon, I was learning that this was not going to be the way to meet my goal of *opening my eyes underwater*. I couldn't do it "drop by drop" but it had to be by "sink or swim" and that meant that I had to beat Karlos in diving for stones and take these competitions seriously.

Friend or no friend.

And that's what I did.

Using the foot method and losing to Karlos ignited the—*pop*! I opened my eyes. Saw the diving stone. Grabbed it and scratched his foot with it.

And never looked back.

Underwater.

Or above it.

I have to emphasize and tell you that learning *Burpese* and opening my eyes underwater happened many years ago when I was young.

It was, however, part of my plan to figure "it all out."

I'm still doing that.

4. **Understanding the Federal Reserve Bank:**

The Federal Reserve Bank system was born on December 23, 1913.

Ernest was born on July 21, 1899.

He was thirteen when the Federal Reserve Bank system was born.

Same age as me now.

I'm not sure if he knew what was going on with the Federal Reserve Bank.

I'm sure he had other things on his mind when he was thirteen.

Or if he cared.

Or if Ernest knew that the president at the time was Woodrow Wilson.

(Woodrow was a pretty racist guy, BTW!)

Or if he cared.

I care about the Federal Reserve Bank.

Mostly because no one really knows what the bank is and does.

But somehow it is always in the news.

All I can figure out right now is that it is a bank for the banks.

And that it is part of the federal government.

And that they make rules.

That's the real reason why I care about the Federal Reserve Bank system.

Anything that makes rules interests me.

School rules interest me.

And annoy me.

And make me laugh a lot of the time.

Some are okay and are good.

I get the whole fire drill rules, for example.

And the one person talking at a time in class thing. Okay, cool.

Also, no cuts in the lunch line.

Who makes rules?

Why?

For control?

Out of fear?
For order?
To keep order?
To find order?
To order order?
May I take your order, please?

Me, Campy/poetry from a quiet corner.

The Order of Beauty

An orchid does not require a lot of water.
It has a place on the table.
Its pages of white leaves are read
as the order of beauty.

Too much water and
its pages cannot be read.
Its beauty will be gone.
That is the order of beauty.

~ C.A.M.

Order: The School Handbook

Does any kid actually read the school handbook?
Or even know where their copy is?

I love when teachers say, "You know, it says in the school handbook on page 42 under Student Dental Rights that you can't floss in class."
That's forty-two more pages than I've read in a book that I can't even find.

Only repeat offenders need a school handbook, anyway, so an administrator can point out to them how they screwed up.
Again.

Repeat offenders.
Recidivists.
The same students.
The group never gets bigger.
It can, however, get smaller because even some of these students shed their slug exoskeleton at some point.
A few.
It is, of course, volunteer shedding.

A free sample from my school's student handbook since you probably haven't read yours (or can find it)

Hapworth Middle School
Student Handbook Rules:

Section I—STUCON: Student Conduct—Gum (and/or Paper Wad) Chewing

Rule 87—STUCON-3645: If a student is caught chewing gum, the following protocol or procedures will be followed:

- **Step 1:** Student will be asked to remove gum from mouth and place it in a tissue or scrap piece of paper and then throw in a trash receptacle.
- **Step 2:** If a student is caught chewing gum a second time, the student's parent(s), or guardian will be contacted with a phone call or an email.
- **Step 2a:** If the student is caught chewing gum a second time and if that gum is found to not be sugar-free, the student's parent(s), guardian or dentist will also be called on the phone or emailed.
- **Step 3:** If the student is caught chewing gum a third time, the student will be assigned to do a PowerPoint on the origin of chewing gum and present it to the class in which the student was caught in the chewing act.
- **Step 3a:** If the student is *instructed* or ordered to make a PowerPoint on the origin of chewing gum, the student will be required to watch one's own PowerPoint at the same time it is presented to the class.
- **Step 4:** If the student is caught chewing gum a fourth time, the student will be required to make a power point on how the development of gum chewing in the world has contributed to the rise of climate change in Malta.
- **Step 4a:** If the student is required to make a PowerPoint on how the development of gum chewing in the world has contributed to the rise of climate change in Malta, the offending student and parent(s) and/or guardian will be required to watch the PowerPoint at the same time it is presented to the class.
- **Step 5:** If the student is caught chewing gum three or more times and has already made at least two or more PowerPoints that the student and parent(s) and/or guardian also had to watch, the student is required to learn Maltese.
- **Step 5a:** Required: Find a teacher or private tutor who teaches Maltese.

Author's Note: There is no known connection or correlation between Maltese and *Burpese*.

A School Banner or Flag

If your school doesn't have one, consider yourself lucky.

If it does, I can just about guarantee you that the graphics on the banner have one or more of the following four things:

1. your school mascot
2. a shiny red apple
3. a yellow #2 pencil
4. two or three books with primary color covers and no writing on them.

It's like the explosion of technology never happened when it comes to graphics on school flags or banners.

So, beneath your school banner, grab and take a hold of your student handbook. It will be a religious and sacred moment.

A student handbook is actually more sacred to teachers and administrators than any religious texts and is equivalent to and probably more holy than the Avesta, the Bible, the Four Books and Five Classics, the Guru Granth Sahib, the Kitab-i-Aqdas, the Koran or Quran, Mahayana Sutras, the Tao-te-Ching, the Tibetan Book of the Dead, the Torah, the Tripitaka (Pali Canon), and the Vedas and the Upanishads combined along with any notebooks of atheists or agnostics that you may know. I also include any sacred texts of Wiccans if there are any.

If I left out a holy text for your religion, belief system or non-belief system or got something wrong, please write me and let me know.

After all, I'm only thirteen and I'm trying to figure out my own life so I haven't been able to get to all the holy texts in the world.

Not yet, anyway.

But if I am able to get my school counselor to drop science or math from my schedule, I'll have more time.

Me, Karlos/Math Head.

Plant the stupid tree, Kro. So what if it's easy. What's the big deal? Sometimes you just get in your own way. Stop thinking so much.

Cut the crap!

Me. Kro.

It's not that easy. I mean it sounds like it's easy—plant a tree. Big crappy do!
If it were that easy, Ernest wouldn't have put it on the list.
Write a book—now that has some meat to it.
Plant a tree? What do I need? Gardening gloves? A trowel? A shovel?

I've gotten this far so I know there has to be another meaning.
Something more.
And I can't do it until I know.
Otherwise it's just crap.
Okay, I might be overthinking this a bit but if I've bought in this far, I'm going all the

way.

Ernest, you better not be crapping me!

I know, Mr. Bloom.
Too many mentions of crap.
An example of bad repetition.
Distracting, I know.
Or, should I use a more similar and descriptive swear word?

Me, Campy.

The type of tree is important. It can't be any ol' tree. I asked my mom and she suggests a pink dogwood or a ginkgo tree. I don't think you're a pink dogwood, Kro, so I'd go with the ginkgo.

Kro grows a ginkgo. Perfect.

But, you should just do it. Bring some beauty into the world. A tree is about as close to a sense of majestic and permanent beauty as you can get unless it's chopped down to make room for a parking lot. Oh, my god, now I'm starting to sound like you! ☺

Why not enjoy the tree and watch it grow as soon as you can? Trees are amazing living things. Be positive.

Me. Kro.

It's not the tree; it's the words.
In a way, it's too simple. I know that and that's the big deal of it.
Ernest was not simple in his thinking so what was he thinking?

Sometimes words become too important.
They become slogans and then people stop thinking and just start believing them and do stupid things.

Slogans can be dangerous.
People hide behind them.
True, Mr. Bloom.

People have done terrible things in the name of slogans.
Arbeit macht frei.
Work Makes You Free.

This slogan was on top of the entrance to Auschwitz, a concentration camp from World War II and other concentration camps, as well.
Work didn't make the prisoners free. They mostly didn't get out alive and were killed or worked to death.
And they certainly weren't at a camp.
Slogans can simplify things too much.
People can do terrible things and give it a slogan.
Terrible things.

In God We Trust is the official slogan or motto of the United States.
It's on every piece of American money.
So what happens if your almost uncle visits and gives you five bucks as a gift just for being a kid and you lose it in your room the next day?
Where is God?
Can you trust God to find your lost five bucks?
It can get deep, I know.

Me. Poet/maybe.

Rage on—

Can I do it all, Ernest?

There's no time to rest

my mind at all

as I keep hitting the wall.

—sometimes this whole thing is bigger than me.

—Kro

Yoda?

Is there a whole Yoda thing going on here that I'm not getting?
Am I trapped in a vortex of metaphor diarrhea?

Maybe I've forgotten stuff I learned from Mr. Bloom's class on how to infer and read between the lines.
Or, Ernest, maybe you've figured out that *thirteen* is such a *self-absorbed* age.
Okay, and, maybe, I did learn one thing in HAND which is that the only thing or mostly the only thing that I can think about is that, as a thirteen-year-old, it's about me.
And my world.

Pretty concrete, I know.
I'm trying to move beyond it.
At this age, one is starting to get beyond concrete thinking, as Mr. Basil would say. Wait, am I quoting Mr. Basil again? I'm starting to worry.
I'm in the what-if or questioning stage of my brain or getting pretty close to it.
I mean, what if Ernest's four challenges don't mean a thing?
Will planting a tree grow hair on my chest?
Or, at least a moustache for me?
What if I don't become a man at the end?

I mean there is so much to do just to keep a non-slug pulse alive while in a school that, well, maybe, reaching manhood is just not worth it.
Not now, anyway.

But what I'm learning is that I have to *think* when I write this book.
Now I'm not against thinking—a hard thing to do in world surrounded by slugs, mind you, but thinking for a book can be intense.
Sort of like running an 880 of the mind that never stops.

It seems the more you think about stuff the more or less black and white it may seem.
Or is it more magenta?
More aquamarine, perhaps?
Fishhook green? (My color combo invention!)
Choose and place *your* favorite crayon color creation here: _____
Crayon colors and real life.

Now. Patience.

Epiphany.
Best vocab word ever.
Fireworks, please.
A drum roll wouldn't hurt either.

I couldn't plant the tree before now.
Before this moment.
First of all, everything that I have ever tried to plant dies.
Not that I've planted anything more than the top of a carrot in a peanut butter jar lid and filled it with water and then forgot about it.
Or when I stuck two toothpicks through an avocado pit and balanced the pit on the top of a jar filled with water so its backside was hitting the waves.
And forgot about it, too.
I wasn't patient enough to plant anything.
It was like watching paint dry.
It was also like wanting to be in a rock band immediately while knowing one chord on the guitar.
No patience for planting.
I want it to be a tree—tomorrow!

I do think that timing is important.
Timing to know what you are doing.
And, why.

I think I was afraid that I couldn't do it.
I mean it sounds pretty easy, doesn't it?
Plant a tree.
But it's got to have something behind it or underneath it besides cow manure which, Campy told me, can cause root burning.
And it's gotta mean something or maybe what Ernest is saying is beyond me.
Something is missing.
Missing.

Me. Poet/maybe.

Poetry as Form Even if You Can't Draw

Plant what you know.
Know why you are planting.
Know that you are putting something
out there and that you will need to
prepare and take care of it. So it
can stand on its own. Writing
is the same thing. Write
what you know.
Put something
out there in
writing
that you
will need
to prepare
and take
care of.
And
nurture
so that
it will
stand on its own. So it can, too. So you can, too!*
Write from your own experience. Get some experiences,
Ernest would say. Every day. Seek them out. Grow. Get out there.
Create a story, characters, write. And, write some more. Some more.
Plant a metaphor tree.

—Kro Kandle

*An example of *good repetition* for emphasis, to make a point. Got it, Mr. B.

Author's Note: *The poem is supposed to resemble the shape of a tree, not an atomic bomb blast.*

Have you ever been a fifty-year old homicide detective in Manhattan?

Here's the drill: If a kid wrote a story about a fifty-year-old homicide detective in Manhattan, Mr. Bloom would ask two questions:

1. Have you ever been a fifty-year-old homicide detective?
2. Have you ever been to Manhattan? Do you know it well?

The kid would say no to at least one of the questions.

"Then what kind of life experience, what kind of insight or nuance can you bring to the story if you haven't lived, seen or felt it? You don't know the names or descriptions of the people, the buildings or the neighborhoods. What about the color, smells and sounds of the everyday scene or action on the streets? You need sensory language—use the five senses! What about the potential dialogue, speech patterns or slang of the characters? How can you add rich description of the characters and places if you haven't experienced them or been there, really been there?"

Whew!

Ernest, as you can imagine, also has strong beliefs about this:

"When you write," Ernest says, "your object is to convey every sensation, sight, feeling, emotion, to the reader...when you walk into a room and you get a certain feeling or emotion, remember back until you see exactly what it was that gave you the emotion. Remember what the noises and smells were and what was said. Then write it down, making it clear so the reader will see it too and have the same feeling you had.

"And watch people, observe, try to put yourself in somebody else's head. If two men argue, don't just think who is right and who is wrong. Think what both their sides are. As a man, you know who is right and who is wrong; you have to judge. As a writer, you should not judge, you should understand."

And you are the main character in your life.

So start writing about yourself.
And, what you have experienced.

Heavy, I know.

Fantasy Freak

But what if you're a fantasy freak and that's all you like to read and that's all you like to write?

Say you have your character live in a castle on top of a hill in the village of Gronkard, which is north of Yago on the Isle of Chokecherry.

Or, after parachuting from a space capsule, you are stranded alone on an Arizona desert and surviving on giant yucca moths at the foot of cactus-like Joshua trees. The only problem is that you think you are in Arizona but you discover you actually landed on a twin planet of Earth called Sguls!

Or you and a space-traveling friend taking in the various constellation sites suddenly find yourselves face to face with a fire-breathing hippo named Dranby-Glo?

Write what you know?

But these are all fantasies.

Can you still write fantasy?

I'm sure Mr. Bloom would thank you for this inquiry.

As would Ernest.

The envelope, please.

The answer is a resounding *yes*.

You can still write fantasy because this fantasy world is something you *know*.

After all, you created it.

Your characters will live in it.

Mr. Bloom would say to make a pencil stick-figure–like sketch of a map for the village of Gronkard. Put in the castle, the farm pastures, the road and bridge to the villainous kingdom Erosia, the mysterious and the magical forest Timeridon which stands between Gronkard and Erosia.

Be sure your protagonist will know how to get to the village of Yago in order to get help when Gronkard is under siege as the Isle of Chokecherry is hard to reach because of the stormy weather and high tide.

Might as well have the bridge be out, too, over the River Bendemeer.

You need a road map when you write, Mr. Bloom would hammer into us.

But even though you have a road map, you can still change your trip once you are in your story.

And take side trips, as well.

There will be an adventure at every turn, he promised.

Not sure if I've learned more about writing from Ernest or Mr. Bloom.

Certainly different perspectives and side trips, for sure.

Both are influences in different ways about writing.

And, life . . .

Write in school if you can . . . even when you shouldn't.

Writing in school worked for me sometimes.

It worked a lot with Mr. Bloom.

But English teachers like him are few and far between.

I'm still recovering from Mrs. Pencey and the year isn't even over.

And, if she knew anything about what I was writing and why, she'd probably make me sum up the whole book in one fat noun.

I could probably do it in *Burpese*.

Then I'd be happy to share it with her.

So, I'm getting this, Ernest.

I am.

I see what you mean.

Writing a book *compels* you to get your thoughts together.

Get your crap together.

Your ideas.

Your *own* ideas.

The *real* kind.

The kind that you feel in your bones.

The kind that can give you chills because you can't believe they come from you and feel like they are real.

And can't be summed up in one fat noun.

Or inhaled by the horse breath of Mrs. Pencey as she would bend over your desk to give you feedback on your writing until she was able to dissect your writing backward as well as forward while the paper charred from the heat.

Choose one or more from the following: Write for your—
1. self
2. life
3. possible brain growth
4. own storytelling
5. survival
6. entertainment
7. non-slug existence
8. path to personhood
9. satisfaction
10. fantasy life
11. escape from reality
12. creation of your own reality
13. own reason here except if you have triskaidekaphobia

Did I Figure It Out?

Okay.
So, I said I was going to write a book.
I got that going on.

And I am going to plant a tree.
Because I have figured it out and I think that it's more than planting a tree.
Like it's more than writing a book.
Ernest knew this and now I'm figuring it out.
I think.

A tree is something that *you* plant.
You put it in the ground.
But it can't grow unless *you* take care of it.
It's a commitment.

You give it life.
Not in a god kind of way.
More of *if you get a dog, you have to feed it, brush it sometimes, walk it and clean up its poop* kind of a way.
And, most importantly, you have to care for it, love it, teach it, guide it—or else it will be the dog from hell.

Back to my former English class with Mr. Bloom as a lot of thing do—
And, as with a lot of Ernest, I'm getting his whole-life-as-metaphor thing—

- Plant a tree.
- Get out of your own stupid, overthinking, damn head for a minute.
- See how you affect something else and nurture it.
- Be thankful that a tree doesn't crap and that you don't have to walk it.
- You do have to feed it.
- Care for it.
- Guide its growth.
- Protect it.
- Check in on it.
- Don't expect miracles. It will not learn how to sit.
- But it will be there because you put it there.
- And it will be there when you are not there.

Got It

That tree.
I'm going to use it as a metaphor.

I get it now.
It's doing stuff and not getting it which is what I do in school most of the time.
Not *all* of the time
A lot of the time.

It's what my dad calls *spinning wheels.*
And Mr. Bloom calls *going through the motions.*
And what Mrs. Pencey calls teaching.

Ernest, if you've been reading this and, maybe, even listening, you know about my whole slug-theory thing and how the world is populated by them.
I'm sure you came across many slugs in your travels and wherever you went, you seemed to really get into it and try to take it all in, to get it, to experience everything.
Even if it was a tough situation.
Courage is grace under pressure, is what I read you might've said about courage. I like what you said, whether you really said it this way or not.

Part of slug existence is doing stuff and not thinking about why.
Just doing it.
Sometimes that works.
In baseball, you've got to go with a quick reflex to field a ball. If there is thinking involved, it's so fast that I can't even tell.

If you think about throwing or receiving an alley-oop pass in basketball, then you've probably thought too much.
It's a nanosecond of thinking.
Basketball smarts.
Just plain smarts, too.
And lightning fast.

I'm thirteen.
I'm a lot like most thirteen-year-olds.
Pretty good at not thinking about stuff.
Too much.
Just taking stuff in.
Not too much analyzing.
I have about nine years of schooling that taught me how not to think, except for a few non-slug teachers thrown in and a never-read-or-found student handbook plastered on my forehead in each grade.

But something kicked in when I figured out how the world works.

The world is inhabited by slugs and I'm mostly surrounded.
That was an important step.

And then I read about you and the *Four Steps to Be a Man.*
And having a dad who is funny and thinks, too, has helped.
And beginning to learn, just recently, that my mom needs to learn how to get a belly laugh.
And having some good teachers who didn't pick their noses with a #2 pencil when they thought the class was doing quiet independent work and not noticing.
Having two *real* good friends is the middle school equivalent of manna from heaven.

Reading also helps. If I didn't read a lot, I wouldn't know about Ernest.
Or that the Cloaca Maxima was a tunnel built under Rome circa 600 BCE to carry raw sewage away from people's houses.
But only if you could afford it.

It had to be rich people's poop and pee.
Only.

Okay

This might be harder than all four of Ernest's Four Challenges.

Now I have to plant something outside of me and it's going to be a tree.
It's going to be outside of my thirteen-year-old *me-first* self.
It's still hard to believe, though, that there is something out there in the world more important than me and my friends.
I might even be thrown out of official *teenagedom*, as new as I am to the teen numbers, for that last line.
I hope there is no upcoming vote on the horizon for my membership in that not so exclusive club.

And I will watch/help/guide/protect/care as it grows.
In a *world surrounded by slugs*.
In ground and above.

Can I protect it, though?
It might be in for a rough grow.
But could it be a spirit home for a Kro?

Count that last paragraph as a poem.

Plant a Tree

My Four Steps in planting a tree and, just maybe, Ernest would agree:

1. Choose a type of tree.

Choice A: *ginkgo*
Never underestimate the obvious.

I can't decide which type of tree, though.

Campy says ginkgo but I'm not so sure although it does sound pretty cool but it mostly sounds like the phlegm you cough up in the morning when you have a bad cold.

Not going to be easy when you're facing the slug phlegm of the universe. BTW, Phlegm was the name of my dad's first car because it was this really awful green color. Sounds like a great date car to me!

Choice B: *oak tree*
This would be an homage to Ernest because he was born and grew up in *Oak Park, Illinois*.

Choice C: *American hornbeam*
I've been doing my research online and it's a lot more fun to do when you don't have to produce a plagiarized word-for-word PowerPoint to present to the class so the teacher can sit there and pick his pants out of his butt while the students do all of the work during class time with their presentations.

This tree just looks tough! It would also be an homage to Ernest. It has smooth bark and it looks like it has bulging muscles. In fact, its nickname is Ironwood because it would dull axes of early pioneers who *plundered* the land from the Native Americans—had to get that in there.

And, the name *hornbeam* is cool, too. *Horn* comes from an old word meaning *tough* and also refers to a horn (that's tough!) and *beam* is an old British word for tree.

And the envelope, please?

Tough decision but I'm going to go with the—
Oak tree!
Simple. Always best to keep things simple as my dad says.
A northern red oak.
The northern red oak is a very common tree.
An everyday hardy tree.
And it's *handsome* and *grows fast* according to my tree books.
Hopefully, me, too.

2. Find a place to grow it.

My dad's place—no doubt about it.
His two-family house has a small backyard which I can see from my bedroom window.

The Purple Line of the commuter rail runs behind it.
Maybe the rattling and rumbling of the train will be like a lullaby to my tree.
I do okay with this noise.
The tree will do fine.
I don't want to be overprotective.
From the start.
Trees, like kids, can get ruined.
From the start.
Takes a lot to *unruin* that.
It can be done.
Just add plenty of non-slug mulch.
Over time.

It will be put in full sun.
No shadows. No place to hide.
No need to. Right in full view.
For me and others to watch
and care for
its growth,
well-being
and
survival
in
a
world
surrounded
by
Penceys.

And there won't be any risk of drastic shade from a *Flying Auntie with Oversized Granny Panties* hovering over it like a giant balloon from the Macy's Thanksgiving Day Parade.
Or an almost uncle who might want to suck up all of the leaves with his DryVac searching for discarded radio tubes and parts or old padlocks.
Or from a too-tidy mother's saying there's too much *dirt* in the *dirt*.

It'll be safe there.
As best as I can do it.

Ernest wrote a book *Across the River and Into the Trees.*
It didn't do too well when it first came out. Even Ernest didn't always get it.
Although people, today, are reconsidering if this book sucks or not.
It did get pretty mixed reviews.
A surprise for a Hemingway book.
Which makes him more human.
And less myth.
I hope my tree does better than this book.
Maybe I'll do a book about it, as well: *Across the Charles River and Into My Tree.*
I just might.

3. **Once it's planted build a *berm* around it.**
I'll put a berm around the hole of the planting. It'll be around four inches high and it will make it easier to water the tree and help to keep weeds out.
And slugs, too.
And other *encroaching* crawling or slithering slug *pests of thought.*

4. **Water it/let it live.**
Regular rainfall will be enough for my tree except for the beginning.
It already has a lot of what it needs to survive.
Naturally.
Intrinsically.
An instinct to thrive and defend itself against slugs crawling up its immature trunk.

I'll know when to water it.
If the soil is cool to the touch, I won't add water.
If it is warm and dry, I will.
That is my pledge.
Overwatering kills trees.
Underwatering—not so good, either.
The balance. Something I am going to try and find.

Overparenting kills.
Your spirit.
And most living things with appendages and souls.

Underparenting—not so good, either.
The balance. Something a parent should try and find.
If slug skins can be shed.
I think they can.

Underpantsing.
Slug Side Note on Underpants—wear them. Wear clean ones more than once in a while, too! Daily if you can swing it. Try to swing it. Even I'm grossed out by that

and I am fluent in *Burpese* and a *Slugtientist* who can spot a slug kid or teacher at a hundred paces no matter what the snow visibility or heat gradient or strep that is in school air. I may be moving on from my previous stage in life to the next soul-searching and more complex part of my existence but that doesn't mean I'm going to miss doing a riff on underpants—no way! I'm still thirteen!

I'll plant that tree.
It will grow out of me.
Well, not really.
You know what I mean.
I'll be responsible for it. It'll depend on me.
And it's a lot easier to take care of than a dog or a raging, charging bull.
Dropping leaves once a *year* instead of dropping poop at least once a *day*.
Now I have to see if my dad has a *dibble*.
Or *planting hoe*?
But I would much rather drive a *planting machine*.
I know he doesn't have one of those.

The tree will need a name.
And I will make a sign and attach it to a wooden Popsicle stick.
The Leopard.
I know.
Using the name of an animal for the name of a tree.
Sometimes it just *is*.

And there is an Ernest connection.
Of course.
Ernest wrote a famous short story called *The Snows of Kilimanjaro*.
It starts off like this:

> Kilimanjaro is a snow-covered mountain 19,710 feet high, and it is said to be the highest mountain in Africa. Its western summit is called by the Masai, "Ngaje Ngai," the House of God. Close to the western summit there is the dried and frozen carcass of a leopard. No one has explained what the leopard was seeking at that altitude.

I want my *Leopard* to seek new heights.
It doesn't have to explain its journey.
It has to get somewhere.
It has to try.
It will grow.
It will try.
And I started my *Leopard's* journey.

Northern Red Oak in the Right Direction

It's done. Finally.
Tree planted.
Near my dad's house.
Free from contamination of toxins from zeppelin-sized auntie underwear.
And, as best as possible, from slug infestation from too much cleanliness in the world.

I made a small marker near the tree:

> *From Oak Park to this northern red oak,*
> *Becoming a man in four steps is no joke—*
> *Planting a tree, part two, all said and done—*
> *Is it possible I'm Ernest's prodigal son?*

Me. Poet/maybe.

Plant What You Know

Plant what you know.
Know why you are planting.

Know that you are putting something out there
and
that you will need to prepare/take care of it
to stand on its own.

Writing is the same.
Write what you know.
Know why you are writing.
Put something out there in writing
that you will need to prepare—
and take care of it
to stand on its own.

So you can, too.
You can.

—Kro Kandle

Inspiration or Perspiration?

That was a poem inspired by Ernest.

And it could have probably been written for any non-slug English class but it was written for my, well, my last year's English Class.

It was read by Mr. Bloom to his current seventh-grade class.

With my permission.

Very cool, Mr. B.

Non-slug-classroom-navigation note:
When students call a non-slug teacher by the first initial of their last name as in Ms. C., Mr. B., or Mx. W., that's always very cool.

Next

"Ernest, what's next?"

"Fight a bull."

"What the . . . ? Sounds like a lot of bull to me!"

**Part Three
of
the
Four Chambers
of
the
Heart**

—The Left Ventricle—

"Fight a Bull"

You're not a moron. You're only a case of arrested development.

—Ernest Hemingway

What the . . .?

Fight a bull?
A what?
What for?
And are we talking human form like Johnny Kaczerowski or animal form?

Figuring out the *plant a tree* thing is beginning to look easy.

I've read a lot about Ernest and the whole bullfighting thing. I'm kind of an amateur expert on Ernest and all that bull.
Don't worry. I didn't make a PowerPoint presentation on it.
And I wouldn't.

Bullfighting fascinated Ernest.
He loved to go to bullfights.
And he even tried it on an amateur level.

Ernest saw over fifteen hundred bulls killed.
More bull.

He saw his first bullfight in Pamplona, Spain, in July 1923. Ernest took his first wife, Hadley, with him and she was pregnant with his son John. He thought that the bullfight could impress his unborn son.
You have to admit that Ernest had strong beliefs.

And it's also at Pamplona, as part of the *Fiesta of San Fermín*, that Hemingway experienced the running of the bulls, *el encierro*, which has had a long tradition.
And, that's no bull.

Ernest brought *el encierro* to the world's attention.
He was good at doing things like that.
Finding things that he thought were cool.
And letting people know.

His novel *The Sun Also Rises* uses bullfighting as a backdrop.
And *Death in the Afternoon* was all about bullfighting.
It was nonfiction, too.
Ernest didn't mess around when it came to bullfighting.

Karlos doesn't mess around when it comes to guitar.
Campy doesn't mess around when it comes to poetry.
And I'm not messing around in becoming a man.
Trying not to, anyway.

I'm not sure how much time I really have left to write my book, anyway.

After all, Bill Gates already wrote his first computer program at thirteen.

Don't worry if you think you are hearing voices in your head, in a good English class or in a Pencey-type English class. Joan of Arc, when she was around thirteen, was hearing voices that told her that she should liberate France from British rule.

Thinking of running for president of your school? Akbar the Great became the Mogul Emperor of India in 1556, age thirteen.

And, age fourteen?

Is your pizza sometimes too hot to eat?

You can thank Eric Van Paris who, at age fourteen, invented the cooling fork which blows cool air on hot food.

Although I've never seen one or anyone use one.

Ever have frostbitten ears?

Chester Greenwood, of Maine, invented the earmuff in 1873.

At age fifteen.

And Malala won the Nobel Peace Prize at age seventeen.

Although Chester and Malala were both getting up there in years.

It looks like time is not on my side. I really don't have that much time especially that now I also have to figure how to fight a bull.

I hope my best years aren't behind me.

I will finish this book.

And become a man.

At age thirteen.

The world already has a cooling fork and earmuffs.

But the world doesn't have a book-writer-tree-planting-soon-to-be-man named Kro Kandle.

Okay, soon to be *hopefully* a man.

And who was also a *bullfighter*?

A bull is fast and can weigh one ton.

More than Campy, Karlos and me.

Combined.

Throw in Chloe and Zip, too!

It is strong.

It is color blind.

BTW: It's not the *red,* it's the *motion* of the *matador*'s cape. The real reason for the red cape, *capote,* is that it won't show *blood stains* from the bull!

Since a bull is color blind, it would probably think that Karlos dresses well. Not even Karlos thinks Karlos dresses well.

Some people think that bullfighting is inhumane.

Some places in Spain have even banned it.

Ernest saw it as a classic fight between living and dying.

To him, it was great drama.

The ultimate drama.
Life and death.
The ultimate extreme sport, maybe, of his day.

People can see death for the price of admission to a sporting event.
To Ernest, people are attracted to this classic battle of life and death.
Death at a sporting event.
The ending, though, is always the same.
The bull dies.
Whether in the ring or out.

The *matador* must make it look like a great contest.
He has tools you can see and feel: grace, charm, guts, charisma, agility, *guile*.
He has tools you can hold and touch: capes, darts, swords and horses.
And, assistants or helpers who can help him in the bullring.
Picadores, banderilleros, peones, rejondeadores.

I have no assistants helping me write this book.
Solo. Sort of like the bull.

The bull has what it has and nothing more.

At the end of a bullfight in Pamplona, the president of the arena decides if the *matador* should get a *trofeo*—an ear or two and maybe a tail.
When the bull is dead.
 He bases his decision on the cheers or boos and the waving of handkerchiefs from the crowd.

I'm not sure what *trofeo* the bull gets.

Kill Meat

Odysseus handled Cyclops.
I don't think I would've done as well.
And, a bull? Well, first of all, I've never even been to a bullfight. I don't think I've ever seen a bull, really.

All I know about bullfighting is what I know from reading what Ernest has written about it.
And what others have written about what Ernest wrote about.

I'm not sure if I am for or against bullfighting, really.
In school, they drill in our heads to respect other people's cultures and bullfighting is part of the culture in Spain, I guess.
Even though, in school, when it comes to respecting stuff, I see so much disrespect among teachers and teachers with students.
And, students with teachers and students with students.
The list goes on.

It's like Kat McKusker.
In the Hapworth cafeteria, she tries to make everyone in the lunch line feel guilty for eating meat.
"Innocent cows have died for your burgers!" she recites while passing out flyers and running around the lunchroom in her leather sneakers.
And leather belt.
"Selective protest," Karlos mumbles out loud as he enjoys a cheeseburger he brought from home. A cold cheeseburger by lunchtime.

Or Candace Suzuki.
Eating animals is bad!
But kicking leather soccer balls is good?

These are tough calls.
The world is not black and white.
Ernest might say it is.
The strong and the weak.
Brave and the meek.
Life and death.

The world is not black and white. Mr. Bloom definitely drilled that in our heads whenever we were discussing the theme of a novel.
The world is more complex than that.
A protagonist may be evil.
But is he all evil?

Fact: Mrs. Pencey is a Slug-of-the First-Titanium-Degree (highest rank, possible), but even she may go home and be kind to her cat and feed it high-quality tuna cat food or take the mail in for her next-door neighbors when they are on vacation.

People are complex.

Scary but am I getting more mature and feeling *empathy* again or just trying out a Mr. Bloom class truism?

Or, take Mr. Dumplos.

He may pick his butt with a #2 pencil, pun intended, and also shovel the sidewalk in front of his elderly mother's apartment building after a snowstorm.

Just don't shake his hand afterward.

And Mr. Krushon.

This is a tough one to think of a positive side.

As far as I know, he hasn't killed, intentionally and physically, anyway, any of his students and, possibly, some of his farts don't smell too bad.

Possibly.

As for *spirit* kills.

Or *enthusiasm for learning* kills?

That's another matter.

Or the different kinds of conflicts a book can have.

Man vs. man, for example.

Or as Campy likes to say and without being obnoxious, I may add: *person vs person.*

That actually makes more sense.

So I'll go with it.

Person vs. person.

Ernest wouldn't.

My point is that I'm not part of the bullfighting world. I don't want to see a bull getting killed. Doesn't really seem like a fair fight.

Then again, it might be interesting to see a bullfight.

You know, as a cultural thing.

Even if I don't agree with it.

I'm not sure if I do or don't.

Aren't fish killed as part of the sport of fishing?

I don't know if people complain about that.

Maybe if they overeat on stuffed haddock.

And, Ernest?

You see the beauty in bullfighting.

It's a life-and-death dance between an animal and a human.

I *get* that.

But I'm not going to be able to fight a bull.

Because I don't get it *that* much. Not yet, anyway.

Life Is Complicated at Thirteen

I can't even imagine what fourteen will bring but it probably doesn't matter since I'll be a man by then.

Unless the bull beats me!

Fighting a bull—for Ernest or for me?
Not sure.
It's a *conundrum*.
Another great vocab word, BTW, if a vocab word can, indeed, be considered great.

I'm not even a huge meat eater, anyway.
True, no red meat for me.
Not because I don't believe in killing animals.
For food, that is.
It's just that cattle cost a lot of money to raise and it takes a lot of the environment to raise them.
And they eat a lot of grain.
So why not eat the grains directly without the middleman?
Or middle animal?

I'm a food *flexitarian*.
Some chicken.
Not a whole lot.
No fish or any seafood of any kind.
Not even tuna.
It smells and I don't want traces of mercury seeping out of my pores and eye sockets.

Me, Campy/poetry from a quiet corner.

No words needed

My dog looks at me with big, nearly charcoal-colored eyes.
I look back and I can see her soul.
It speaks to me without words.
A wag of a tail, a look that says love and loyalty more than anything else.
I see her love for me, my family, for life.

I feel her spirit when she walks in my room.
I see her spirit when she runs ahead of me on a walk in the woods,
      always looking back to be sure she is not too far ahead.
      Or that I am not too far behind.

Her thick, curly brown and white fur helps to hide her on the trail.
It protects her wild ancestors but that is really my job.
To keep her soul, her spirit, alive in the world with me—
      not too far ahead
      not too far behind
         but in my heart—

         in the middle of my heart.

~ C.A.M.

Me, Karlos/Math Head/Numbers Poet.

How many hamburgers in pi?

You are welcome through my house's front door,
Yes, enter freely, especially if you're a carnivore.
Except for Zip, we're definitely not vegetarians.
But, all are welcome, we're strictly nonsectarian.

The number of hamburgers eaten here is pi so far,
Pull up a chair, we'll count them at our hamburger bar.
No pity here for cows except those patties served at school.
Hamburgers with real meat are delicious and that's no bull!

—K H-L W

Find the Bull

Okay, bull is everywhere.
Especially at Hapworth Middle School.
But a live charging bull?
Well, I know where I can find it in human form.

Is *fighting a bull* going to drive me completely crazy like *plant a tree*, Ernest?
I don't even know where to find a bull, anyway.
Sometimes I wonder if you actually weren't writing for a modern thirteen-year-old boy in pre-manhood?

Now a *virtual* bull?
That'd be easy to find.

I have a funny feeling I am going to have to look further.
It's just part of the *ambulance driver in battle*–type adventures life that I'm seeking.
Isn't it?
As if navigating and fighting the halls of Hapworth aren't challenging enough.

Got Adventures?

Get adventures.

My dad, when he was a kid, did stuff with his friends with this in mind:

Create adventures so you can talk about them when you get older. That's not the whole point of having adventures but it's one.

In Ernest's case, he had adventures and wrote about them.

Me, too.

I feel that Ernest thought you could learn more about life if you put yourself on the line with adventures.

As much as you can.

I agree.

I'm still not fighting a bull.

My Writing and Ernest's

This is the most writing I've ever done in my life.

Longer than my thirty-three page short story in fifth grade.

Longer than a list of complaints my mom has about the cleanliness of the house on a normal day, if possible.

Longer than Auntie Melba's list of underwear outlet stores in all of New England.

Longer than my almost Uncle Dewey's to-do list on parts he needs to bring his old radios back to life so he can listen to weather reports.

Longer than Mrs. Pencey's checklist for the TKAM essay on how literary devices are used.

I've actually learned a lot about my writing from doing this book and I wrote a big part of it in Mrs. Pencey's class. I did enough of her required writing to suck up and get a decent grade but then I'd get right back to my book, to what really mattered to *me*.

Not a bad way to learn.

Ernest learned a lot about writing in the short time that he was at *The Kansas City Star* newspaper.

What have you learned in your two million years of schooling?

For Style

The Kansas City Star had a style sheet—rules that reporters should follow when they wrote articles for the paper.

Ernest thought that *four* of those 110 rules were most important to him.

The Four Writing Rules according to Ernest and *The Kansas City Star*:

1. **Use short sentences:** Hemingway was famous for his short, concise sentences. He didn't believe in flowery language. I'm sure you, or kids you know, use a thesaurus when you are writing for school. I'm sure Ernest didn't.

2. **Use short first paragraphs:** A reader isn't going to hang around long enough with your writing if they have to plow through a *ginormous* opening paragraph or two.

3. **Use vigorous English:** I think this is when an (anti–Mrs. Pencey) English teacher would say "show don't tell." I'm guessing you might have heard it. If a character in your story is learning to ride a bike for the first time, let the reader see, feel and hear the challenge, the grunts, groans and cheers as well as see and experience a scraped knee or two with a lopsided flip to the side. Then, that moment when the rider on the bike is finally going it alone, the thrill of feeling free has to be felt, not told about. I think you get it. *Be present.*

4. **Be positive, not negative:** Ernest was not a sweet-talking, look-at-the-roses kind of guy. I think we've established that. So what does this mean? It means that instead of saying what something *isn't*, say what it *is*. Instead of writing that something "isn't cheap," try writing that "it costs more than he wanted to spend" or instead of "that team's passing in soccer stinks," try "The team could work more on its passing."

5. **Watch out for slugs:** In life and in writing. Number five is mine, not Ernest's but I think he would agree and so would *The Kansas City Star*.

Questions

I wonder if Ernest asked a lot of questions growing up.
Or, was he just looking for answers.

Quo vadis?
Ms. Kazakh, my Latin teacher, would often start class with this.
Like, what's going on?

I threw in the *like*.
Not sure if it works in Latin, anyway, or if there is an equivalent translation.

Someone once asked Mr. Krushon a question during one of his no-take-a-*halitosis*-breath-lectures.
Krushon was startled to be asked a question during his step-by-step-never-vary-from-the-point-until-the-last-student-is-passed-out-from-sheer-boredom-and-exhaustion-and-spins-off-the-sides-of-the-Earth-and-is-reported-as-eternally-missing-from-any-kind-of-learning.
His whiteboard marker dried up on the spot.
So did he.
On the spot.

Big Eternal Questions of the Slug Universe.
There are more than five.

1. Guessing what Auntie Melba's underwear size is takes me into infinity numbers.

2. Asking my almost Uncle Dewey questions about tubes for old radios in order to distract him from mowing my hair with his car vac buys me time *and* my hair but it doesn't really advance my thinking and/or place on this Earth.

3. Telling the difference between *effect* and *affect*.

4. Wondering if anyone really reads the nutrition signs and food plate or inverted food pyramid posters plastered all over the cafeteria.

5. Trying to figure *things* out and questioning instead of just going for the *ride* and being booted up from one grade in school to the next.

   Kids can flunk most of their classes in middle school and still be promoted.
   Promoted to nowhere.
   Being promoted to a new grade is easy.
   Thinking about the next grade in your life – not so much.
   As you know.

   Kids need a plan to survive *slugomotions*.
   If they don't have one, they might think about getting one after reading this book.
   Could be.

Why Do Some Kids Suck?

Kids who bully, by definition, suck.
Already I broke one of Ernest's four writing rules—*write it positive.*
This is a harsh statement, I know.

It doesn't take into account any background like if the bully kid had a bad hangnail on the day of their worst bullying tirade or the frustration from the night before when they couldn't find the TV remote and that they had to take it out on the kids sitting at the third table from the lunch line door in the school cafeteria or if there was some humiliation felt when they noticed huge underarm sweat marks showing on their fancy T-shirt or that their new mega-expensive signature sneakers got scuffed so they had to body check the second-smallest eighth-grade kid into the lockers during passing time.

Otherwise, kids who do stupid things do stupid things because kids do stupid things and maybe, just maybe, they'll learn from them and promote themselves to the next grade of doing stupid things.

Why do some kids bully other kids and even try to bully slug and *even* non-slug teachers or at least their classes?

Slug-bully kids often can't tell the difference. The slug teachers, though, don't really deserve it even though they might be bullies, too. *No one* really deserves it but it's the non-slug students who end up *paying the price* for the bullying of teachers, both varieties, as well as the bullying of other students.

It does suck.

Some kids, the ones who suck and bully, conduct a reign of terror throughout their slug school careers.

You can probably recite a list of names right now!

When they leave one grade for the next, all of the teachers already know about these kids coming up to their grade.

I've overheard teachers in the hall talking about these kids.

They are *The Teacher Whisperers.*

Some whisper louder than others.

Do they really think that kids aren't eavesdropping?

Do they really not notice that when another teacher visits another teacher in a classroom and they start whispering about something the whole class will suddenly get deathly quiet so they can hear what they're talking about?

Kids have big ears.

Even if they're not that big, all kids have *big* ears.

They might not hear a word that a Pencey or Krushon is saying as they do their slug drill sergeant bit in front of the class, but they can hear what two teachers are whispering about at a hundred yards.

In great detail.

Not forgetting a word.

When some teachers are whispering together in front of the class, kids are actually listening and that may be for the first time in that class.

Teachers Talking to Teachers.

Teacher-whispering conversations are most active during the following times of their lives: the planning of vacations, the discovery of new smoothie recipes or the addition of any kind of home improvement like a new kitchen, bathroom or a backyard deck so they can barbecue or grill the remains of their slug souls with a side dish of slugstatium, known as Sl with atomic number 124 on the periodic table of elements and a dash of slugferfordium, known as Sf with the atomic number 125 on the slugeodic table of elements.

Too long of a sentence, I know.

Teacher Whisperers in these categories will, roughly, barge into the room of the teacher next door or to the room of their nearest teacher friend, during class time, I may add, with frequency hovering nearly 3.768 times a day.

That's an official estimate in a world surrounded by slugs.

Kids love these visits.
They then have the following five amazing and wonderful options:
1. Shush other kids to get the class quiet and try to eavesdrop.
2. Space out.
3. Get homework from other classes out of the way.
4. Read a book. (It could happen and maybe the book could be this one.)
5. Talk (quietly) with their friends.

With number five, though, things can go terribly wrong.
As only they can in a school.
It follows the "Do as I say, not as I do" rule of school life.
And slug life.
So, while your teacher, during class time, is talking with a teacher friend about how their newly renovated basement gets puddles of water after a big rain, you get busted for turning around and asking Sanjay, who sits behind you, if he'll lend you a dollar so you can pay back Casey who lent you a dollar the day before.
With twenty-five cents interest.
School Economics 101.

BTW, teachers can talk with other teachers about anything they want during class.
Just make sure I can't hear you.
It affects my concentration when I am doodling.

It Happens.

Some teachers have *it*.
Some don't.
You know what teachers have *it*.
And what teachers don't.

I'm not sure that *it* can be taught when a wannabe teacher goes to college.
There has to be some innate talent.
To *do stand-up*, that's what Mr. Bloom calls it, in front of a class and make it interesting.
At least most of the time. Even Mr. Bloom had his, well, deep sleep-inducing-moments.

For example, you can practice a sport that you like.
For hours and hours.
But, to begin with, you have to have *some* talent for it.
Otherwise you don't get to the next level.
But you can still play it and have fun, get some exercise, hang out.
And you're okay with being at the level you're at.
No NBA in your future but you have a decent crossover and can dunk your brother's
Little Tikes basketball hoop.
And talk some trash.
And look like a baller!

But, if you're a slug teacher who is just okay with their borderline amount of talent for
the *stand-up* in front of the class and can't, won't or don't care about getting to the next level, it
sucks for everyone.
In that classroom.
In that school.
In your head.

"A good teacher has to have a good stand-up," shared Mr. Bloom with Karlos and me
during one of those after-school hangout times with a teacher which can sometimes be more
interesting and have a more powerful impact than any other time with a teacher.
An example of incidental learning, Mr. Bloom adds.

Okay, I get that not all of a teacher's time is spent in front of the class.
Mr. Bloom says it's called being "the sage on the stage."
But being funny helps, by the way.

Even a little bit funny.

Bully Promotion

The current teachers who have the slug-bullies in their classes can't wait to promote these kids to the next grade.

Okay, they can't wait to get rid of them.

The receiving teachers in the next upper grade hope that they don't get them in their classes.

And the students, who have been with these *SBs*, *slug bullies*, for years, are just used to it.

They're resigned to their fate in life.

SBs get to roam the halls, come late to class, not do homework and be fresh to the teacher.

Or any adult.

And there's always an umbrella of drama that follows these *SBs* around.

Always.

There is real danger, also, when a parent of a bully is called into school.

And, that can be pretty often.

Run when you see a bully-and-parent combo enter your school.

Don't walk.

Run—

in the halls,

up walls.

Keep running.

Hide in lockers before you're stuffed in one.

There's no sheriff in town.

Your principal will fold.

The local authorities should be contacted.

The school counselor will hide under their desk eating M&Ms.

And the bully-parent-duo will slog through the halls in Godzilla-like-fashion.

Eating the younger and smaller children in their wake.

Stuffing the younger and smaller children into lockers.

Students running and screaming in every direction like the worst horror movie you've ever seen.

WWED?

What would Ernest do?

What would Ernest do if he saw a slug-bully-parent-child combo heading toward him in a school hallway?

Well, Ernest did have some experience with wildlife.

The Wild Life

Ernest was a big game hunter in Africa of animals like lion and antelope.

Okay, he only spent ten months in Africa, but the continent did have a big impact on him and he did survive two plane crashes and physical problems that could fill up a year's worth of hospital TV shows: first-degree burns, a concussion, crushed vertebrae and a ruptured kidney, spleen and liver.

He left Africa with some big game trophies—you can debate the merits of big game hunting when you write *your* book.

It was a different time.

I think you can say that big game hunting was a metaphor for Ernest.

And for me in this book.

Try to stay with me if you can, even if you don't think you can get past the big game hunting part or maybe big game hunting is cool to you.

But here it is—it's about *going after something*.

It's about taking something on.

It's about staying with something.

It's about *doing*.

And *doing* it well.

And *completing* the challenge, the job at hand.

And completing it well.

Okay, I know what you're thinking.

What kind of challenge is it going after big game with a Springfield rifle?

Metaphor, my friend.

Big game hunting is a metaphor.

Think about it.

A great prize.

A great challenge.

The need to be smart.

In so many ways.

Okay, the Springfield big game hunting rifle was needed which didn't do great things from the animal's point of view.

But it was the adventure, the goal, the plan, the quest, the hunt and, okay, the trophy.

Remember, it was a different time way back then in the preorganic era of history.

I don't think they had all of the food allergies in those days like there are today, too.

We're going to be serving antelope patties at Little Timmy's birthday party. Is anyone allergic?

BTW: *For the record, I am opposed to all big game hunting but I am for all metaphors.*

Me. Poet/maybe.

Nuts to You

Everyone's allergic to something.
No more random food binging—
Milk, nuts and chocolate—
Add slugs to the list—don't forget!

—KRO

There's Something Write About It

When Ernest wasn't in the middle of or recovering from the physical disasters he had to endure, he had some great experiences to write about.

The stuff leading up to the physical disasters were experiences, too.

As was surviving them.

He believed big time in, as you know, write what you know.

What you experience.

And you can use this for a fast fact—

He wouldn't run if he saw an adult slug bully walking down the middle school hall with their young.

No way.

Or if the slug bully cub's parent were walking alone.

No way would he run, hide under a desk eating M&Ms or squeeze into a locker, or two.

Or let the *SB* or *SB* cub rule the hallways.

The lunchroom.

The school.

Ernest had guts.

And when the writer Dorothy Parker asked him, "Exactly what do you mean by 'guts'?"

Ernest replied, "I mean, grace under pressure."

Grace under pressure.

Again.

Ernest, I think this might be where you really said the 'grace under pressure' thing.

Cool.

Still works for me.

Out of My Head

I tried the *grace under pressure* thing after I tripped over one of Auntie Melba's oversized panties that was being used for the bathroom doorstop and crashed into a wastebasket jammed with used Q-tips of her dried ear crud which spilled onto my bare feet.

I didn't quite master the *grace under pressure* after all that happened.

How come some kinds of hassles only happen within families, like being contaminated with loose ear crud? Is it because a kid has more contact with their family so it's a playing-the-odds kind of thing?

When do a kid's friends take over in more importance from the members of one's own family?

Or maybe friends don't but serve as a substitute.

Sort of like butter and margarine.

Sometimes I literally am hovering over my family and have to wait for them to catch up.

I then come back down to Earth pretty quickly, sometimes.

Only to start flying around again.

Get balance, I know. Balance.

As you can see, I'm on my flight path in life.

Ernest never mentioned anything about flying a plane as far as I know.

Probably better.

With my luck, I'd probably have to fly Auntie Melba and almost Uncle Dewey five hundred miles away to the nearest fast food buffet restaurant because she has a half-price coupon and inside her travel bag, which she stores right next to me on the passenger seat in the cockpit, would be her tarp-sized underwear which could double as a parachute if needed along with a small travel kit of Q-tips that she has already used in flight along with an opened-up deodorant stick with teeny fossil remnants of shaved armpit hair.

Although, if I dumped her travel bag in flight, it could prove to be another great terrorist deterrent.

"We give up! We give up! The clouds are raining used Q-tips with crusty ear crud and what appears to be an unidentified auntie and almost uncle from New Hampshire! We love your country!"

The *friends* thing is the part of the whole independence teen-primal-urge-stage, I guess.

You know, when you start distancing yourself from your family to make your own identity.

And part of every thirteen-year-old's *weltanschauung*.

Fun to say it out loud: *velt-ahn-shou-oong*

German word that means someone's world view or perception of the world.

Cool word, Dad. Thanks.

Did you see it earlier in the book? Did you look it up?

I know, probably not. No worries. Now you know. When you use the word, people think you are swearing or not sure at all what you could be talking about! A great word to use incorrectly:

Coach, I hurt my weltanschauung. *I won't be at practice today.*

What the weltanschauung *do you think you're doing?*

How long have you had that problem with your weltanschauung?

Weltanschauung! *My locker is stuck!*

Excuse me, I'm looking for a blue weltanschauung *in my size.*

A word that can multitask.

Me, Campy/poetry from a quiet corner.

I, Too

I, too, am the girl from two worlds.
I, too, write of America in black and white.

I am the khaki-colored daughter
Who eats pasta dinner with my large Italian family
When Aunt Christiana comes,
And we tell stories.
And eat too much,
And grow sleepy from the meal.

Tomorrow,
I'll be at Mom's family's table
When Uncle Curtis comes.
Everybody'll care
And say to me,
"Eat your shrimp and grits,"
When.

Together,
They see how beautiful I am
And are proud—

I, too, am America.

Thank you, Mr. Langston Hughes, for *writing the way*.

~ *C.A.M.*

Weltanschauung **Alert**

I am not going to quit school and become a volunteer Red Cross ambulance driver in Europe for two reasons.

The first is that I don't have a driver's license and the second is while I think it could be a good career move for a writer, I'm not sure I can afford to be a *volunteer* anything if I move to Europe by myself. Being a volunteer Red Cross ambulance driver did, though, give Ernest a lot of great life experiences.

It worked out pretty well for Walt Disney, who was a volunteer Red Cross ambulance driver in World War I, too.

Script

As my dad says, *Life has no script. No one knows the story line being written of one's life and you're in the middle of your own story.*

Heavy, I know.

And you're more than in the middle of my story.

And, that's no bull.

Which is the hassle I'm facing.

In *my* script.

The Slug Credo of Hassles

Slugs create a hassle when none is necessary.

And hassles, while not surprising, are usually unexpected.

Especially if they could have been avoided if there were an anti-slug venom available that one could take to stop the inevitable hassle before it happened.

Or a slo-mo camera that could slow down the hassle so you can do something to stop it, avoid it or just step back and watch it implode—at a distance.

Preventative survival tactic one: *Always expect the unexpected.*

To quote my dad and, coincidentally, Mr. Bloom. Ms. Kazakh said it in Latin, too.

Actually, I don't remember how to say it in Latin.

Not even sure if I ever knew how to say it in Latin so Ms. Kazakh probably said it in English when talking about Julius Caesar.

Or some other dictator.

Preventative survival tactic two: *Always create the unexpected. In a good, anti-slug way.*

That's my motto.

I think it's a gut reaction from when I would be shocked from seeing Auntie Melba's *SuperSize* granny underwear and bras, made from recycled all-season tires, that were washed in the sink and hung up on the shower-curtain rod to dry in the bathroom.

What did I create from that eye-shocking and traumatic situation?

I created a belay by tying them together so I could rappel out the second-floor bathroom window for emergency air supply.

You do what you gotta do.

Talk about a hassle first thing in the morning when all you wanted to do was brush your teeth.

Me, Karlos/Math Head/Numbers Poet.

Sure

Sure, eat a peanut butter sandwich while using my computer—
See if I let you use it again in the future.

Sure, bug me while I'm reciting pi at seventy-two decimal places—
You are very lucky that you can hide behind your braces.

Sure, pull the cord out of the amp while I practice—
You will be so left off my first rock concert's guest list.

Sure, spill grape juice on my Pencey essay that was on my desk—
I'll be downstairs waiting for you to confess.

Sure, be annoying when Campy and Kro are here—
Why do you have to be so *little bro* in overdrive high gear?

—Karlos

A Ton of Bull

A *bullaton*:

Okay, if a bull weighs a ton it can't be easy to hide but I've never ever seen one.
I've never even been to a bullfight.
All I know about bullfighting is what I know from reading what Ernest has written about it.
And what others have written about what Ernest wrote about.

I've decided I'm one hundred percent against real bullfighting that may be going on in today's world.
In school, they drill in our heads to respect other people's cultures.
So there must be a culture in some countries that likes bullfighting.
And I bet that even in that country they can't agree.

When Mr. Bloom taught us about the different conflicts in literature there wasn't, and this is an homage to Campy, *person vs. bull*.
Nope, never saw that one.

But there should be this: ***person vs. bully***.

Person vs. Bully

Epiphany!
That's it!
I think I got it!
Person vs. bully is *it*.
Ernest, what do you think?
I think it works.

Ernest wouldn't say *person*, would he?
But this is about *me* becoming a man in four not-so-easy steps.

He would call it *man vs. bully*.
As I am currently in the pre-man step number three, I am going to take the bull by its horns (sorry about that!) and call it *person vs. bull*.
Of course, I owe sincere thanks and incredible amounts of appreciation and lunch cookies for this push to Campy.
You help more than you know.

I, the near-man, am going to *fight the bully(ies)* wherever they may lurk, hide, slither, pounce or incubate.
No problem.
I think.

And get extra credit, I feel, for fighting *slug bullies*.
Which they all are by definition.

Cyberbullies

"Cowards. They are all cowards," Ernest would have most certainly said. "The worst kind of predator."

Bye-Bye, Bully Culture

The culture of a thirteen-year-old can be and feel mysterious, special, elusive and exotic for the uninformed.

That would include, possibly, everyone *over* thirteen.

And under 13.

One could say, however, that if a person is over thirteen that there is a high probability that they can claim to have had the experience of being thirteen and might have some knowledge or awareness of the experience.

I wonder what odds Karlos would put on that.

It's time.

In Kro-13-year-old-Kulture, I'm going to fight a *bull-y*.

Name the place and time.

Any place. Any time.

That works for me.

It has to work for me.

Because the culture around bullies is just plain wrong, stupid and, don't forget, pretty *funny*, too.

Remember that!

And what I have learned about bullfighting from Ernest applies to fighting bullies.

Fighting bullies, also, will keep me busy for a long time.

A long time.

Even with help from Campy and Karlos.

The kind of bully fighting I'm going to do is not the kind with capes, darts, swords and horses.

But the kind of fighting with grace, charm, guts, charisma, agility and *guile*.

The same qualities that you, Ernest, admire in a *matador*.

I'd also throw in humor.

Can't hurt.

I have read all that you have written about bulls and bullfighting especially at Pamplona, Spain, and it has helped, Ernest.

El encierro, the running of the bulls in Pamplona, has taught me about *fighting the bully*.

To survive *el encierro*, it's imperative to *know* the course.

Really know the course.

For your safety and survival.

Because the bulls are chasing you down the streets and alleys of Pamplona to end up at the bullring.

Just like bullies who jam their way down the hall to get to the cafeteria first so they can get their food and be knighted and seated at the cool table in the cafeteria.

Know the halls.

If you're a *new* runner in *el encierro*, the wider the road the better. This helps you from being trampled by the bulls *and* the other runners. That way, if you need to, it's easier to duck into an alleyway or doorway.

This is especially useful information for when you are between *City Hall Square* and *Mercaderes* in Pamplona.

Probably, and as no surprise, the most dangerous part of the race is in the beginning.
Everyone is a bit unsure and anxious.
And excited.
This part of the race starts from a corral and leads into the *City Hall Square*.
You'll be running a steep angle.
And, the bulls are closer together.

Bully(ies) tend to do that.
Run close together.

The metaphor here is, in case you missed it, and it's no fault of your own, *to know the bullies.*
Know the course.
Know the bullies.
Know their moves.
Study them.

Why?
First, it's really fun.
And, funny.
It's *anthropology*, seeing how bullies behave in groups, in society.
Where they habitat and gather. (Not even sure if *habitat* can even be used as a verb. I might've made that up.)
How they clothe themselves.
What tools they use.
Why they do what they do.
Or don't do what they don't.

Me, Campy/poetry from a quiet corner.

No, Emily, we were never a nobody

I'm somebody, who are you?
Are you the queen of the school?
Then there's one of us—who's not!
It destroys us, you know.

How dreary to be the cool queen!
How better to be a friend.
And share the halls the entire day
To the school year's end!

~ *C.A.M.*

. . . Emily Dickinson, you are somebody to me.

Me. Poet/maybe.

Still I Rise, the Son

You may cut me in the cafeteria
With your first-in-line food high,
You may think of me not worthy
But still, like the son, I'll rise.

Why do you cover your gloom?
You see, I am just starting to bloom.
'Cause I listened to Ernest and myself
Instead of lies in the classroom.

Just like writing a book and planting a tree,
With my eyes on the prize,
Just like being born on the Fourth of July,
Still I'll rise.

Did you think that I am always joking?
Bowing down with despised eyes?
Weakened by your cool kid lies?

Does my vision of a slug offend you?
Don't you play the cool kid card?
'Cause I write poetry like I've got a voice
Hangin' far from the cool kid bar.
You may throw words with your food,
You may push kids in the halls,
You may kill them with your insecurities,
But still, I'm the son, I'll rise.

Does my confidence upset you?
Does it show that I am wise?
That I read like I'm after treasure
So I can learn all with my eyes?

Out of eras of history, bad things can happen.
Did you rise?
Up from classes that discuss right from wrong
Did you rise?
You are a sea inside turning to storm,
Crashing in turmoil, can you reach the shore?

Leaving ahead nights of stars and clear
I rise
Into a journey that is a to-be-a-man frontier
I rise
Bringing a gift from Maya Angelou to share,
I am strong to myself when all else seems unfair.
I am the son.
I rise
I rise.
I rise.

—Kro Kandle

. . . *Thank you, Maya Angelou, for the inspiration.*

Me, Karlos/Math Head/Numbers Poet.

What happened to the white chickens, William?

so much remains
on the

name tag of
today

scoured with soap
water

in front of cruel

children.

—Karlos

. . . We share the name, William <u>Carlos</u> Williams

Bully Anthropology 101: Lunch Table

What is their habitat? Where do they gather? *The cafeteria.*

Okay, they clog up the halls, too, by being hunters and gatherers for their social lives.

But it is the cafeteria that is their home base. To be precise, it is the *cool* cafeteria table, or two, that can be in any section of the lunchroom. It depends on the school. If you're homeschooled, it could be your kitchen table so don't, again, think you're beyond this whole 'being cool and a bully' thing because you don't have a cafeteria in your house. Get over yourself.

If the cool cafeteria table has only ten places to sit—this is an estimate; individual seating may vary at your school or home kitchen—there will be a natural swelling and/or overflow of self-identified cool or popular kids to sit at and be seen at that table or two.

Seen by whom? That's the (free) entertainment part! No one really cares about them.

Just *them.* They look at each other.

Know the course.

Their goal? To be seen or be part of the cool table(s).

They will be, after bullying (and stampeding!) their way into the cafeteria to get a seat at the cool table(s), grabbing a seat, trying to double up and share a seat if they have to and sitting on laps until a teacher, administrator or lunch aide tells them that they can't double up. It's a whole *musical chairs* kind of thing for the self-identified cool kids during eighth-grade lunch.

I don't even want to think what the soundtrack could possibly be.

If they can't get a seat or double up, they will stand around the table and be floaters. Again, this behavior lasts only till an adult catches on and intervenes. Unless the adults, too, want to curry favor with the cool crowd and casually look away.

Know the course.
It's so interesting to watch them.
Because they want to be watched.
Not only by one another but by you.
But you should watch with a smile on your face. It's funny stuff.
The cool lunch table as metaphor.
As metaphor: *preening, strutting bulls.*
Know the course.

The cool kids may possess potential bully qualities. This is a fact because to be cool and to get a seat and keep it at the cool lunch table requires some *slug-bully moves* such as:

- *Plowing down* an unsuspecting student as you race to get to a seat at the cool table.
- *Running over* an unsuspecting student as you race to get to a seat at the cool table.
- *Smashing into* an unsuspecting student as you race to get to a seat at the cool table.
- *Acting fresh* to the teachers or aides who are on lunch duty in the cafeteria.
- *Not cleaning up* the lunch table after finishing eating.
- *Being seen* in the uniform of the cool kids at the cool cafeteria table.
- *Looking to see* who's looking at them.

Bully Anthropology 102: Clothes

I guess we all dress in our own uniforms in our own way.
Karlos— under the radar but he's got his own style of not having a style.
Campy—unique style of putting fun and mismatched things together that is only Campy.
Me—whatever is mostly clean and I like to think that, yes, I have my own style. Still working on what it is, though. Ernest made no mention of clothes or fashion as far as I know.

The bully clothes? Never unique.
Cookie cutter all the way.
They stampede like, well, bulls, to get in certain mall stores to buy their uniforms.

Do they ever wear red?
Do the research.

Bully Anthropology 103: Tools

Their most cowardly (Thanks, Ernest, for the perfect adjective!) tool is a computer or a phone.

Or the newest and greatest technologically advanced version of either one.

And, of course, the Internet.

Their other tools are, usually, what they all think is cool for the moment which usually starts from what someone else or some company thinks is cool and can pass it on to them.

If one slug bully (*SB*, for short) has something or thinks something is cool or wears something that is supposed to be whatever they think is supposed to be cool, then whatever that is that is supposed to be cool will spread like *slug wildfire* to all of the *SBs* in your school or at your home.

As a cautionary tale, slug wildfire is dangerous to most living things but, unfortunately, *SBs* are not aware of the danger to themselves.

Very sad.

But it can be a lot of fun to watch, too.

Just don't get too close because you might get burned.

Know the Course

Running with the *bulls* and surviving requires knowing the course.
Running with *bullies* and surviving requires knowing the course.

Know the course.
Watch them.
And ignore them at the same time. That *really* hurts them.

It's not *their* school.
It's not *their* space.
It's where *you* are.
The school isn't called *Slug Bully Middle School.*
Or, *Slug High School.*
Or, even, *Slug Elementary School.*
Okay, and, *Slug Homeschool.*

Know the course.
Because it's your course.
Your school.
Not theirs.
Don't give up the ownership of the halls, the classrooms, the grounds—everywhere.
Know the course.
And, as they migrate in the halls, watch them.
As they watch themselves.
Stare at themselves.
And as they fake answering questions because they are not prepared for class, it's fun to watch! Some slug bullies do well in school, surprisingly. I think it's because they can play the game which requires little original thinking. They're trained in that. Gut-thinking is not in their repertoire.

Having non-slug teachers can help, too, and that might be the biggest challenge of all but seek them out.

They are there.

Spectator Sport

Unlike most sports, *Slug Bully Watching* requires no special, extra or costly equipment.
It's an inexpensive sport. Free, actually.
And, it's fun.
A fun spectator sport because you really don't want to participate.

A good workout can be had by all if you track the Slug Bullies.
Good tracking skills involve knowing their scents because whatever is the most "now,"
marketed and advertised body wash/cologne/smelly stuff/perfume to tweens and teens, that is
what they will be wearing.
Follow the scent.
They smell.
Alike.
Even to their shampoo smells.

And, continue to know the course.
It's entertaining.
Watch their preening and dating habits.
It's amusing.

Know the stretch of the bully course between *City Hall Square* and *calle Mercaderes* that
is necessary for survival.
At *Pamplona Middle School.*
At your school.
Know the alleyways and doorways.
Know the classrooms and school hallways.
Know the bus stops.
The locker room.
And, always know who *you* are.
And who you are becoming.
Huge.

Talk Your Game

Good verbal skills can come in handy.

Taunting a slug bully gets you nowhere.
Calling a slug bully names is a waste of time.
And could be dangerous, too.

But, in the event of a slug bully approaching you in *pure slug-jerk mode*, it's always good to be able to spar with witty and clever words.

That being said, it's probably best to ignore them and further develop your *observation* skills as the slug bullies are there for *your* entertainment.
For *your* free entertainment.
And they don't even know it.

Show Your Artistry

You don't look at the death aspect (the outcome of death for the bull in bullfighting): but you look at what happens before that, at the bullfighting, where you slow the bull down, you break the bull and once you have done that you can try and show your artistry in front of the bull. It's always been said that a bullfighter cannot know fear, only respect. Let's say that someone who is fearless—if you are not afraid of something it is because you don't know just how dangerous it is, and that makes it . . . you are not afraid, it is a crazy thing, isn't it?

—Luis Mariscal, a matador, talking to Robert Elms, in Bullfighting Aficionado

Your artistry can come in many forms.

- Respect the slug bully? Not sure about that. Never fear them. Be careful around them but never fear them. Luis and I agree about that.
- Ignore the slug bullies.
- Know that they are there for your entertainment.
- They don't know that. Makes it more entertaining.
- Be witty, if needed.
- Never be in attack mode.
- Ignoring and being entertained = best path.
- Get a non-slug adult to inform or help if the Slug-Bully Behavior gets weird or creepy.
- That can happen.
- Enjoy *la corrida*.

Pass the Salt

The best physical answer to a slug or Slug-Bully Behavior is to pour salt on it or on them.
Putting salt on a slug causes them to dehydrate.
It's kind of the opposite of osmosis in their bodies.
All of the liquid in the inside of the body goes to the outside.
And it looks like they are melting.

> In the movie, *The Wizard of Oz*, the Wicked Witch of the West is melting and cries out as Dorothy watches: *You cursed brat! Look what you've done! I'm melting! melting! Oh, what a world! What a world! Who would have thought a good little girl like you could destroy my beautiful wickedness? Oooooh, look out! I'm going! Oooooh! Oooooh! I'm melting!*

I'm not suggesting pouring salt on a human slug.
I do use the word *human* loosely in this regard.
But, in your mind, if you could sprinkle salt on them, poof, the slug behavior would be gone.
And so would the slug hassle.
How cool is that?

Salt can be a metaphor.
Carry invisible salt with you.
NaCl for the soul.
You'll feel better.
Metaphors can be very powerful.
And not just for school.

Bullies will never go away from Earth.
We lost dinosaurs but we won't lose bullies.
Sad, I know.
So, never leave home without *salt*.
Without your *metaphoric* salt.
Okay?

Choose Friends in Slug-Polluted Air

Bottom line, here is the best thing to do in the face of Slug-Bully infestation in your school, your house or on the orbiting planet that you may inhabit. No doubt about it. No two ways about it. This is it: *Don't go it alone.*

I'm not.

Have at least one good friend. If you are reading this and if you don't have one good friend, get one. Bottom line.

Have a friend or friends to share in the sport of *Slug Bully Watching*.

There are no merit badges earned for gaining expertise in this. No merit badges are needed. Doing this with a friend or friends is enough.

Two good friends.
Campy and Karlos.
In a world surrounded by slugs.
So I'm doing okay.
So far.

Know that—
- Bullies will never go away from Earth.
- Always know the course.
- And never leave home without salt.
- Keep laughing.

I'm fighting the good fight, Ernest.
Good idea.

Next

"What's next, Ernest?"

"Father a son."

"Not again . . . !"

Part Four
of
the
Four Chambers
of
the
Heart

—The Right Ventricle—

"Father a Son"

The shortest answer is doing the thing.

—Ernest Hemingway

Me. Poet/maybe.

Advice to me, a young poet

Never prepare

to be a man

unless you know the four things beforehand

and don't put a vacuum hose on your head to clear your mind.

—Kro Kandle

To Martín Espada:

Your poetry motivates me to write.

Me. Poet/maybe.

*Rap*prochement

Man, Ernest, I don't understand what you're telling me now.
Following your four-things-to-be-a-man was my solemn vow
to make my eighth-grade grade quest to manhood in re-al-i-ty come true
for my get-out-of-jail-free card and no ad-o-les-cence curfew
but I took this leap of faith without knowing all; I was listenin'
to you while seeing home movies of my life reminiscin'
and I think maybe this is a trick and I'm your rabbit out of the hat
while you knew there's no escapin' my mom's home and Hapworth hab-i-tat
and that everything is as it is, nothing else really matters
as I crawl over this Grand Canyon clinging to a shaky rope ladder
because what I am trying to clearly know, grow and comprehend
is that here's not what it seems and don't know what's around the bend
and I'm tired, weary, wary to go deeper 'cause to get past each gatekeeper
of a man-challenge on this Metaphor Road keeps getting steeper.

—TwoK

Checkered Flag

You've made it to the fourth and last section of the book. I can't even believe that I've made it this far.

You can't either, probably.

The question remains: Am I going to be able to get through this fourth and final section and challenge?

Father a child?

Ernest? C'mon, man.

How much can *I* change?

Word Value

There is a shock value to words.

I know Ernest knew of the power of simple, direct words: Father a son.

Probably, though, in defense of him, I was probably not his target audience. I'm not sure if his *Four Things to Do to Be a Man* were designed to be PG-13 or way above my age group like, maybe, mid-thirties.

Or mid-twenties, at least.

But Ernest, as far as I know, never put any age requirements on those who read his work so I'm going to have to figure out the *metaphor route* on this one—big time.

As my dad says, *KISS—Keep It Simple, Son.*

A good way to lead life.

Except the usual translation of it is this: *Keep It Simple, Stupid.*

Or, Mr. Bloom's version when it comes to our writing: *Keep It Simple, Student.*

Ernest says it simple in words but to do it isn't simple at all.

Like the writing of this book is a bit like riding a wild horse.

Or, better yet, a bucking bull.

I'm going to try hard as hell to stay on and I know I'm going to be thrown off, too.

Simile.

No fun to be thrown off and sometimes, really, simpler to stay off.

Much simpler.

So, what is it going to be, Ernest?

Oh, wait, I'm pretty sure it's up to me, right?

Free the Moustache

I've gone pretty far, Ernest.
Farther than I really thought I'd be able.

For more than a million reasons, and you probably know most of them, it's not going to happen – father a child.
No way.
No how.
Not now.
I'm thirteen.
And I haven't even kissed a girl yet.
And, as you know, I've written that my hope and dream of kissing a girl is to go into it moustache-free.
From the girl's point of view, that is.

I know there is room for a metaphor here, Ernest.
I'd even settle for a simile.

Me. Poet/maybe.

I sing the moustache electric razor

I sing the moustache electric razor,
because the teeny hairs of those I love enrich me and I nourish them,
They will not be shaved off till I see them, respond to them,
And be able to count them, and trim them full with the charge of my razor.

Was it doubted that one day I could not grow a moustache, then reveal you,
And if those who defile my being able to are as bad as they who rumors spread all?
And if the moustache does not do fully as much as a bare cue ball?
And if the moustache should not be mine first, a kiss is still my goal.

—Kro Kandle

For Walt Whitman
Man, you had a great beard, sideburns and a moustache!

Slacker

And, just for the record, by the end of this book, if I make it, I'm aiming for *enlightenment* with a small *e*.

No sense in shooting too high.

I'm thirteen.

Book or no book.

Ernest or no Ernest.

I still have a lot of slacker in me.

Sorry, *Siddhartha*.

Bathrobe: The Will to Live, Eat and Write

I'm writing this sitting up in a chair.
Usually I'm at my desk in my room or at the kitchen table.
At my dad's.
Or my mom's.

I seem to write better at my dad's.
When Auntie Melba is over at my mom's, the smell from her cooking makes my brain corrode because she is always sticking her fingers in and tasting it and I can't ever get out of my mind the one time I accidentally saw her naked leaving the bathroom because she couldn't find her robe after taking a bath.
So it's hard to concentrate and write.
Let alone eat there.
As you can imagine.

That she couldn't find her robe which is the same size as the infield tarp at Fenway Park is still hard for me to believe. Auntie Melba always buys things that are extra-large, even table napkins, soup spoons and trash bags. "More roomy that way," is her usual response.
And that I *instantly* didn't go blind *on the spot* (Mr. Bloom, again, would say, "Do you see the redundancy here?") when I saw her is a testament to miracles still happening in this world on planet Earth.
And it's why I get a bit queasy, to this day, when I see the infield tarp rolled out at Fenway Park during a rain delay.

Auntie Melba, a Girl Once?

My sister Chloe didn't need to be in my book.

She's okay and everything but I'm in a totally different space than she is.

She's smack dab in her girlhood and I'm leaving my boyhood and entering my manhood and, according to my calculations, I'm seventy-five percent there.

Me using *percentages* and not in school!

Who would've thunk, Ms. DuFarge?

Life does work in mysterious ways.

My mom, she's not a girl, of course.

Female, yes.

And I'm guessing that she has had some experience as a girl, of course.

She wasn't born a mom but she's not a girl.

Anymore.

What does she know about kissing without a moustache?

And, what would I ask her, anyway? "What's better? A kiss with or without above-lip follicles?"

She would have nothing to compare it to.

Auntie Melba.

A girl once?

Well, I know she had to be young at some point.

Her youth had to happen.

Although, if I didn't have Mr. Krushon for science, I could ask a science teacher.

I could ask Ms. Ibraheem.

Even if you weren't in her class, you could go up and talk to her and ask her a science question.

Or about her March Madness bracket.

Very cool.

I'm sure, against all odds, though, that Auntie Melba was a girl once.

Or at least young.

It's logical.

Logic can be scary.

I've had girl teachers.

Okay, women who are teachers. Some great teachers, too.

Ms. Kazakh. She rocks!

Would have loved to have Ms. Ibraheem for a science teacher.

Ms. DuFarge?

It was a setup for her right from the beginning.

I hate math.

Just hate it. (To be totally honest—I didn't hate Ms. DuFarge. It was really a *math thing* only. It was a setup for disaster from the very first integer.)

And, because in this section I am headed closer to manhood than ever before, she made math class tolerable 41.68 percent of the time. Not a bad percentage when dealing with an anti-math student like me.

Okay, there were plenty of times when she could have eased the math pain and she didn't. She just didn't.

If you weren't on the Brain Math Track, to her you were kind of invisible. Or so it seemed to me. The trick here is that, unbeknownst to her, I could have probably done Brain Math.

Really.

And tested well enough to get into the advanced brainiac class.

If I cared.

One thing I know about myself in the two stages of my life, so far—*before and after Ernest*—is that I'm not a math fan.

No way.

So, in the self-examining days that I am in right now, 59.32 percent of the time I zoned out in math.

Out. Way out.

But I was writing some good poetry in math class.

Free verse, a sonnet and a villanelle or two.

And some great doodles of computers and old-school rotary-dial phones—both my favorite things to draw during the time we were supposed to be checking our work.

And, Mrs. Pencey?

My one-word analysis about learning anything about anything from her, let alone anything in English class—*no.*

End of short story.

Her girlhood? That's how the Headless Horseman lost his mind!

A school counselor from non-slug heaven? Yes, it is very possible and probably true that Ms. Chen was a girl once.

And then she retired.

Lot of nerve for her to retire and leave us.

Why do the best former girls have to leave?

Me. Poet/maybe.

Checklist

In order to be a man
get to the next level and
live by one's own plan
born of Kilimanjaro mountain.

As I make the man-plan work for me
to know I'm earning my man degree.

Epiphany—
for me.

—Kro Kandle

Me, Karlos/Math Head.

Kro, you'll probably be able to grow your own moustache by the time you're thirty if you're lucky.

Hopefully, then, people won't just think your upper lip has some dirt or Pop-Tarts crumbs on it.

Thirty might also be about the right time that you would be experiencing your first kiss anyway, so at that point, the two moustaches would cancel each other out.

I know I'm not sounding like much of a friend, but trying to find a girl who might like you and would want to kiss you or to play out the odds here, that the two of you would possibly want to kiss each other at the same time, is a lot to deal with at once and is pretty unrealistic. I mean who would want to kiss you anyway besides your dog? So, throwing in the part about the girl not having a moustache might be asking a lot. You're not exactly the heartthrob of Hapworth, you know.

I mean your friends like you and that's about it.

Bottom line: If a girl gets a moustache before you, go with it.

Omba Yamamoto

Omba Yamamoto sits next to me in English class.
I like her.
She's a girl but our relationship revolves solely around me borrowing paper from her and the occasional *Wite-Out*.
And, I admit, I stare at her in class a bit.
Okay. A lot.
Mostly because she reminds me a lot of Campy.
Not looks-wise but style-wise.
Omba's not someone I'm going to approach about how to figure out this fourth *Ernest challenge to be a man.*
Borrowing lead for a mechanical pencil doesn't invite a conversation on boy/girl stuff.
But it does get me thinking about the possibilities.
No moustache, either.

I wonder if Omba likes a man of action?
I'm not quite the Red Cross ambulance driver in World War I–type of action man but I'm right in the middle of it when it comes to the action at Hapworth Middle School.
Not the cool action, mind you.
The *everyday kid* kind of action.
Maybe, just maybe, could Omba be the one?
The lucky one.

I mean compared to Ernest, this kiss-a-girl thing could be easy, kind of, sort of.
Ernest had *three* sons.
Four wives.
I am going to kiss *one* girl.
Still not going to be easy.

Problem is who is it going to be?

Or how?

Whoever it is, I've got to let her know.
She's officially part of the last step for me to become a man.
She'll need to know.

We'll need to like each other and probably start dating.
Not even sure how to go on a date.
Or what to do to get to that point.
And, hopefully, not being a complete or even a partial jerk in any way.
Or any kind of a slug.

Life: complicated again at thirteen.

Pondering a Daydream

I'm still sitting in English class.

And Mrs. Pencey is thumping the whiteboard and reviewing literary devices so she can further ruin TKAM.

For those of you who have forgotten everything in your schooling or in this book so far: TKAM = *To Kill a Mockingbird*.

My mind is elsewhere as it often, okay, always, is with her class.

I liked reading TKAM, actually. Pretty powerful stuff.

Just that now it's going to be ruined.

Officially I'm in a daydream.

I am trying to think about my new manly life.

Looking at Omba.

But really thinking about Campy.

Where is she this period? What is she doing? What is she thinking?

Hmmm, Sherlock?

Connection?

Whenever I think of Campy, I also think of Karlos and me. We are definitely a threesome.

I guess we're a *clique*.

Or a *three-ique*.

Is that bully behavior?

To be part of a clique?

I don't think so in this case.

Nobody's *in*.

And nobody's *out*.

And while I always liked Karlos.

And I like Campy.

I'm thinking that maybe, just maybe, I really like her in a way that I don't like Karlos.

As in *like*.

You know exactly what I mean.

That's why she is a good choice.

And this might work.

In a daydream, first.

Of course.

Daydream: No Experience Necessary

Karlos has less experience with girls than me.

He's not much help right now except, when I'm over at his house, he plays some loud guitar riffs which help me think.

It's the sound track of my daydream.

My dad is being supportive of my quest, as much or as little as I've shared with him, to kiss a girl, but he's talking about me asking Campy out for a date.

Old school.

But he does want to have "the talk" with me.

Again.

He's not in this daydream.

Neither is my mom.

Kiss a girl?

Like a girl?

To her it would be one step before Campy and I elope and are stowaways on a freighter heading to Pago Pago in American Samoa.

Math fact so my mother won't freak: By my calculations, the average length of a romantic relationship in the eighth grade at Hapworth Middle School is nine days which evens out to almost two school weeks with one full weekend smack dab in the middle. The weekend is good for starting a relationship but between classes is the best time, by my observations, to end a relationship. You can always use the excuse after you drop the break-up bomb that you're rushin' to Krushon's class and can't be late!

Because you'll lose points.

Which you already did.

By being in that class.

My Daydream: This Is It

My daydream is brought to you by the actual, everyday usage of a partial, as needed, alphabetical list of literary devices as taught to me by Mr. Bloom, already, when I was in seventh grade, BTW, but I have to suffer through the review of them again with Mrs. Pencey. You can probably tell that I'm bored to death, and sweating, resulting in excessive underarm perspiration odor in her class. And that's an understatement.

Oh, and a big sunspot-shaped sweat stain under both arms.

Huge.

I guess Mr. Bloom was right.

He said, "You never know when you'll use or need literary devices in everyday life as well as in an English class, in any kind of writing or even in a conversation!"

I doubted him, for sure.

But if I can use one to reach my fourth and final step to be a man, then what the hell.

I have a lot invested in my manhood at this point and I don't have anything else to lose, except just that.

And, what better place to use or lose literary devices along with the hard work that I have so far put into my manhood than in a daydream?

Not sure because if it's in a daydream, does that mean I am really using them or not?

But daydreams can become real.

Or, so I am told.

My daydream starts now—
If it works out in my favor somehow, I hope reality takes over.

alliteration:

Me. Kro:

The literary devices, selected somewhat randomly and presented in an unfinished alphabetical order, are in the *foreground* in my daydream with the voice-over of Mr. Bloom narrating each one with examples from my life. I can use the help in presenting these and, plus, I'd rather him do literary devices than Pencey. He also has some life experience which could come in handy.

The point of view, then, is in third person omniscient—Mr. Bloom. He's all knowing.

The words, though, are actually *mine*.
They're supposed to be, anyway.
It is *my* book, after all.
Again, complicated.
BTW, I'll sneak in some of my own narration in my daydream.
And, my forever apologies to Mr. Bloom because his words might sound very much like me since I wrote them and he can't change them.
Omniscient, or not.
I hope.
I guess if he's all-knowing, he can do what he wants.
But it's still *my* book.

Mr. Bloom as daydream narrator:

Welcome to Kro Kandle's daydream. I, Mr. Bloom, will narrate this part of Kro's odyssey and his interpretation of the *Four Things to Do to Become a Man*, according to Ernest Hemingway.

So, here it goes.

Kro is figuring out, or so it seems, that he likes Campy.

Will Campy also consider that she may, coincidentally, like Kro and possibly contemplate and/or consider, at some point, that they might care for and concurrently like each other?

Me. Kro:

Those are my words?
Whew—too much alliteration even for me.
And it's my daydream!
Daydreams think of stuff that is wilder than real life.

I do like that Mr. Bloom is being direct on my behalf.
Being this direct doesn't always work in real life, does it?

allusion:

Mr. Bloom as daydream narrator:
    Who else but a celebrated poet from the Victorian era to capture the true romantic feelings of our modern-day Odysseus and adventurer, Kro Kandle. Here is a sampling of her most famous love lines:

> *How do I love thee? Let me count the ways.*
> *I love thee to the depth and breadth and height*
> *My soul can reach.*

    —Elizabeth Barrett Browning
        (Sonnet 43, *Sonnets from the Portuguese*)

Me. Kro:
    Love?
    Making a reference to a *love* poem, Mr. Bloom? I think he's going *uber*-English teacher on me.
    I'm just figuring out that maybe, just maybe, Campy and I are more than friends.
    Maybe.
    Who knows?
    Or that I can walk her home from school.
    Without Karlos being there.

    Already it's complicated.

anecdote:

Me. Kro:

Mr. Bloom said that an anecdote is a brief story that is often funny about a certain incident in a person's life, and we heard a million of 'em from him in seventh grade.

Make that a million and one.

Mr. Bloom as daydream narrator:

So, Kro and Campy—check out that brief alliteration, by the way—were walking home from school one day. Karlos stayed after for the rehearsal of the Hapworth all-school musical of *Grease.* Yes, the school performed *Grease* three years ago. Get your tickets early, they go fast!

As they were walking home together and each lugging what seemed like fifty-pound backpacks, Kro accidentally, casually and lightly, bumped into Campy.

He was trying to get a reaction from her.

He did.

"Why do you keep bumping into me?" she asked with a puzzled look on her face.

The dating rituals of two thirteen-year-olds.

It must be noted that it's not clear nor has it ever been chronicled what exactly the dating rituals are of two thirteen-year-olds.

Anthropology.

autobiography:

Mr. Bloom as daydream narrator:

I remember the times when I was thinking of my friend Campy as, well, um, more than a friend. Being thirteen at the time, it was pretty much trial and error. Karlos, my other best friend, was about as much help as holding on to an anvil during a swimming meet.

How was I going to go from friend status with Campy to, well, a different, undefined *status somewhere beyond friend?*

"Uh, excuse me, Camp," I nonchalantly mumbled under my breath as I gently hockey-checked her into the shrubs lining the sidewalk.

"What the heck was that all about?" Campy grumbled as she picked brambles off her sweater and backpack. "Walk straight much?" she glared.

The plan was obviously not working.

How can I perfect accidentally bumping into her every five paces as we walk? She's going to figure out a pattern here.

"Kro, is the planet spinning too fast for you? You're walking a bit weird!"

My plan is not only not working but I have no plan B except for waiting till age fourteen for my first kiss.

That puts my manhood on hold, too.

I don't think she'll ever know that I might like her more than a friend.

Ever.

Me. Kro:

Ouch!

Pretty painful scene for me to witness in print.

biography:

Mr. Bloom as daydream narrator:

     Kro thought that because he was thinking about Campy in a somewhat different way that, magically, somehow, this cosmic vibe would be transmitted through the Gulf Stream air and arrive, serendipitously, at her front doorstep as she, too, had miraculously been dreaming of this moment her whole eighth-grade life and age of thirteen.

     And, because of Kro's sending these messages out to the universe, she will pick up on all of his signals. If she misses any of them, like Kro slyly bumping into her while the two of them are walking home from school, then all that is lost is that she thinks that he is a big-time klutz.

     The cosmic question of the universe remains, however. What if she never realizes that Kro likes her a bit more than as a friend?

     Never.

     Would all be lost?

     Forever.

Me. Kro:

     Ouch squared! The pain of it all!

     I think I'll need to rewrite Mr. Bloom's narration.

     Another cool part of being a writer—

     You are god.

     Small *g*.

     But still god.

character:

Mr. Bloom as daydream narrator:
Kro's character in his book is the protagonist. After all it is his book and he's writing it. It's something he is compelled to do by Ernest and others.

Most importantly, by himself.

You know the drill—the journey to overcome challenges, to search and find oneself, to test and uncover one's core and destiny like the quests of Odysseus, Katniss Everdeen, Cassie Logan and Frodo Baggins.

Among others.

While Campy is, clearly, an important character in the book and, of course, an important person to Kro, she might be considered a minor character as she casually comes in and out of the book which is also a metaphor for Kro's mind.

Me. Kro:
Campy, minor character?

Not to me.

Mr. Bloom, if that were the case then I wouldn't have my heart set on well, you know . . . .

Mr. Bloom as daydream narrator continues:
Being a minor character is not an insult to Campy or Karlos, either.

The three are good friends and one of the three wants to be more than friends with one of the three.

Karlos is not part of this particular picture.

conflict:

Mr. Bloom as daydream narrator:

The types of conflicts in *running with slugs* by Kro Kandle are ripe for debate in English classes the world over.

In my reading of his book, I would say there are at least two main types of conflict in regards to his quest to become a man as well as fulfilling the fourth "Hemingway" challenge, in particular, to kiss a girl, which is Kro's metaphor for 'father a son' and to have a "dating" relationship with Campy and that they "like" each other. Whew, exhausting, I know.

You, the reader, may agree or disagree. No one really agrees on what the meaning of life is so why should people be expected to agree on a story, on literature which is from life, directly from life?

The first conflict I see is *person vs. self*: Kro vs. himself.

It's not like a conflict in boxing, pro wrestling or ultimate fighting but a struggle with himself, within himself. It's a struggle to get from one level to the next, from one place to the next, from one stage of development to the next stage in order to meet that last challenge of Ernest's *Four Things to Do to Become a Man*: To explore what it is like, perhaps, to like someone and, possibly, that *someone* may like the person back and whether that may lead to a kiss.

Another conflict for Kro would be *person vs. person*: Kro vs. Mr. Dumplos *and* his contaminated #2 pencils!

An additional conflict could be *person (Kro) vs. society*: Kro vs. the society of slugs and slug culture according to him.
Kro cites the following signs of slug culture:

- Mr. Dumplos
- Mrs. Pencey
- Mr. Krushon
- Auntie Melba's eight-person/two-room tent-sized granny panties (her moustache, too)
- Student handbooks
- The slug feeling when a student is assigned to get the slug teacher of a subject and not the non-slug human-being teacher of that subject
- The slug "Do as I say, not as I do" of teachers and adults
- The lack of people teaching and speaking Maltese in the schools and homeschools of today
- Homeschoolers who think they are exempt from slug teachers and slug rules and slug air
- School counselors who aren't Ms. Chen

- Tidy sock balls
- No Burpese taught as a second language in schools and homeschools
- Slug bullies—adult and kid sizes
- The Slug Essence that can be in the school air
- Lunch lines

If Kro can figure out how to continue to survive in a society conflicted and surrounded by slugs, will he—in the end, or is it the beginning—be able to kiss the girl?

While not being a slug in any of its many forms, shapes or patterns.

By doing the right thing.

By asking her.

And possibly have more than a nine-day relationship.

Dramatic tension is everywhere.

dialect:

Mr. Bloom as daydream narrator:
Maybe I, Mr. Bloom, did something right or maybe it's just Kro. His book is mostly written without extra *likes* sprinkled in nearly every sentence in the way that many kids speak today.

Maybe writing is a way to counter the proliferation of using *like* in kid dialect.

Manhood might be, like, around the corner.

dialogue:

Mr. Bloom as daydream narrator:

It was a typical after-school afternoon mid-April if there could be a typical after-school afternoon in middle school, as Kro would describe, in a world surrounded by slugs. Karlos was still in school as this was the big day when the actors in the school musical, *Grease*, rehearsed with the musicians for the first time.

Kro figured that it was good that Karlos not be there. If Kro were going to screw this whole thing up, better to only have Campy witness it and not the whole world, meaning Karlos, too.

Stopping by Campy's locker in the tsunami-like dismissal rush to the lockers at Hapworth was risky business. Trying to figure out how to go from friendship to more-than-friendship was even riskier business.

Kro knew the scene, however. He knew the delicate balance and weighed carefully and ponderously the pros and cons of what he was about to do. Or imagined doing.

He thought to himself, I have to keep my eye on the prize which is, bottom line, to keep my friendship with Campy.

Remember, it is I, Mr. Bloom, who is the omniscient all-knowing narrator, who can tell you, the reader, what is on Kro's mind or in his mind even if he is not sure what it is.

With all of Kro's pre-thinking of the situation, there was still going to be a lot of improvisation. No doubt about it. Aside from the fact that he wanted to keep the friendship with Campy at all costs, the whole not-make-a-fool-of-oneself is also huge.

Or upgrade this to not-make-an-ass-out-of-oneself is huge.

He rejected the third-party idea of having Karlos investigate or inquire if Campy was, in any way possible, interested in Kro in that way.

Kro also rejected the idea of having Karlos write a note to Campy asking of her interest in Kro being a boy as opposed to just being a friend. This, Kro ended up reasoning, is virtually the same thing as having Karlos ask Campy directly for him.

Kro and Campy headed toward the usual back exit of the school in an attempt to avoid the stampede of students-with-too-heavy-backpacks.

Exiting Hapworth with minimal end-of-day-rush-hour damage, Kro and Campy headed on the walk home.

Kro couldn't think of anything else except *the move* in order to *ask her*. Writing poetry, it seemed to him, was so much easier than using words in real life.

All Campy wanted to talk about was her latest art creation.

"Ms. Ibraheem wasn't in school today and the sub gave us the science work that was left for us to do which I finished in about five minutes so I did some drawings of my dog Governor."

Kro looked at her while she was talking.

The move. The move.

Ask her. Ask her.

He couldn't even hear her words.

"Okay," Kro answered to no particular question.

"So, I also started this long poem and I'm going to make a watercolor to go along with it," she continued without skipping a beat and noticing Kro's weak attempt to be part of a dialogue, let alone a conversation. "And I think it could be an okay poem but you never know."

The compliment route, Kro thought to himself. *Go the compliment route.*

He mumbled out loud, "But you're a great poet, Campy. One of the best if not the best at Hapworth."

"Thanks, Kro. I like doing poetry. I might be getting a little better with it this year."

Tripping over a half-centimeter-high pebble, Kro regained his balance. "What is the poem about?"

"Animals. But not the cute animal-poster kind of poem. This poem talks about how animals have souls and people don't treat them as such."

Animals with souls? Kro felt a slight kick in his stomach. I wonder if she knows about Ernest, he thought. You know, his whole fascination with and respect for bullfighting.

"Animals with souls?" he asked with his voice getting higher than he planned on. "What do you mean?"

"You know, like they have feelings, like emotions. You know how, like, when Governor cries when I come home from school later than usual. She is so happy to see me and she's sad and mad at the same time. That's a lot of emotion," Campy said with great passion.

Awkward silence.

"What do you think of bullfighting?"

doodling:

Me. Kro:

Not a literary device, I know, but it is English class with Pencey so while I am intently daydreaming, I'm also doodling.

Comes with the territory.

drama:

Me. Kro:

In this case, not the middle-school kind of drama but literary-device kind à la Mr. Bloom.

You know, like a theater play.

Like Shakespeare.

What's a good first date?

Going to a movie, right?

Okay, I get it that you have to get someone to go with you first.

I like plays but going to a play with someone, well, that's a little much.

I have nothing against plays but this is my book and I'm taking *dramatic license* here and making this into a *movie script* so it's also easier for you, the reader, to watch in your mind.

It's on the next page.

I needed a lot of room.

Reel Drama: The Movie Script—

EXT. (*Exterior shot*) CAMPY'S HOUSE—LATE AFTERNOON

The front yard has a few patches of brown. New leaves are starting to form from the buds on the branches. A slight breeze is blowing. The sun shines on CAMPY'S house through the new green growth.

> MR. BLOOM
> (V.O./VOICEOVER)
> The well-known line of *April showers*
> *bring May flowers* is originally from writer
> Thomas Tusser and written in 1557. The original
> was *Sweet April showers/Do spring May flowers*.
> What does April bring, this curious month that
> heralds in the new and miraculous of spring and
> life each year?

EXT. A BULLFIGHT as a *matador* dramatically moves his cape as the bull crashes through the open space. WILD CHEERS erupt from the crowd. There is an image of ERNEST sitting in the stands and closely watching.

EXT. BACK TO CAMPY'S HOUSE

KRO and CAMPY are walking up the driveway to the back door of Campy's house. The two casually and slightly bump into one another. They climb the stairs and stand on the porch.

> KRO
> (nervously fidgeting)
> Campy, there is something I have to ask you.

Campy's dog Governor jumps to the glass of the door from inside the house.

> CAMPY
> (reaching for the key to the house)
> What is it Kro? I have to get inside and let
> Governor out and today's the day I have to
> run over to my cousin's house and babysit. I
> only have a second.

Campy opens the door and Governor darts toward her with excitement. While holding Governor gently by the collar, she looks over at Kro and she touches her fingers to her lips and points to Kro's lips.

CAMPY
(with a gentle smile on her face)
May I?

KRO
(with a nervous but happy smile)
Um, yes.

Campy leans over and quickly kisses Kro on the lips.

Kro appears quietly stunned.

EXT. WORLD WAR I BATTLE SCENE

A Red Cross ambulance truck in the background. SOUNDS of battle and war everywhere. Clouds of thick grey smoke and dirt swirl on the ground.

A fallen soldier resembling KRO is picked up by a female AMBULANCE DRIVER and cradled in her arms as he comes back to life with a slowly developing smile and half-dazed look on his face

EXT. NEAR THE BACK DOOR OF CAMPY'S HOUSE

CAMPY turns to go into her house.

KRO
(awkwardly)
Yeah, see you tomorrow.

KRO runs off the porch skipping a step at a time. He runs down the driveway and continues sprinting down the sidewalk. A light shower begins to fall.

EXT. DRIVEWAY LEADING TO STREET

Overlay full-screen photo of ERNEST writing at his desk while KRO jumps and runs home catching every puddle he can.

dramatic irony:

Me. Kro:

Okay, my daydream is ending. I think.

After this *dramatic irony* section, my book goes back to *normal*.

If you're a character in a book, especially in your own book, you don't know that dramatic irony has happened all around you.

You can't know.

It's only the people outside of the book like you, the reader, who know if dramatic irony has taken place because it happens when the audience knows something that the character doesn't.

For example, is this the last literary device used in the book? I'm not sure but I think it is from my perspective, anyway, which is not an example of dramatic irony.

Romeo and Juliet is a good example of dramatic irony: act 5, scene 3. Okay, I was learning a little in Pencey's class, but mostly got this Romeo and Juliet stuff on my own.

I'm not going to spoil it for you in case you have to read the play for school, which can be a slug experience, as you know, with a slug teacher and, especially, if the ending is ruined for you, so I'll leave it up to you to find out why it's a perfect example of dramatic irony and you can even write a paper on it or do a PowerPoint on it.

All I can say is that I wish Juliet didn't drink that potion although it probably made sense to her at the time.

And, when you read Shakespeare, it is okay, as Mr. Bloom points out, to know the plot beforehand which makes the play easier to follow.

So I didn't think I really ruined anything for you with *Romeo and Juliet*. Maybe I even helped a little.

And, man, could Shakespeare write the love poetry:

> Good night, good night!
> Parting is such sweet sorrow,
> That I shall say good night till it be morrow.

—William Shakespeare, *Romeo and Juliet*, act 2, scene 2

I'm not ready to write love poetry—yet. I think I'll save that for my next book and, plus, I have to see how things work out with my Ernest man-plan and, okay, with Campy, too.

So, Mr. Bloom, I'll take over the rest of the narration.

It's a *man's* job and I can do it.

Thank you for pitching in up to this point.

I guess you can say I will be the omniscient narrator, first person, because it's my story.

And that I *am* the omniscient narrator.

Campy kissed me.
And she kissed me on the lips.

I'm pretty sure I kissed her back. I did agree, after all.

If one person kisses you it has to be considered a *kiss back* by the other person because, technically, it takes two to kiss.
Actually, four lips, if you want to get technical.

We shared a kiss.
She must have been thinking about kissing *me*.
That means I'm not the only one.

We shared a kiss.
Not *sharing* in the same way your teacher talks about how lower grade teachers talk about *sharing* and not taking all of the best toys and jamming them into your cubby space in elementary school.
And this kind: "Well, if you're going to bring in _____ (fill in the blank) to class, then you must share and bring one in for *everybody* in the class."
Wouldn't work for kisses.

And not the *sharing* that is talked about in middle and high school as far as sharing your feelings and emotions about troubles that are happening halfway around the world or that the star basketball player has a hangnail and can't play in today's game when no one is talking about problems with kids getting concussions from getting locker doors smashed into their heads.
By the in-house *SBs*.
Or should I say in-school *SBs*.

Sharing *the* kiss, though, is on my mind.
So, it's back to me, I guess.
To *share* a kiss means that there might be other people than me on the planet who are thinking about stuff.
Like a kiss.
A shared kiss.
It could mean that there are more people than me who experience the world or who want to experience the world, in the non-slug sense of the world, of course.

And maybe, probably yes, Campy was thinking about kissing me.
About sharing a kiss with me. She asked and I said yes.
She got it into and then out of her own head.
That's what I have tried to do in this whole book.
Get into and out of my own head.

See what is *out* there.

So, yeah, it looks like I got kissed. Cool that she asked.
Not sure that Campy had planned it for that moment.
But it happened.
There had to be a seed in her thinking.
Which shows that *she* thinks.

I kind of knew that already.
After all, she is my friend.
My friends *think* and I *think* in a non-slug way.
But this was a nice way of showing it.
It does beg the question: Are we dating? Are we a couple? Can we make it to at least nine days and stay friends no matter what? What about Karlos? These questions and possibilities will need to be addressed.
Life, again, complicated at age thirteen.

I did think that in this universe surrounded by slugs that I was trying to figure out, that I was the only one who really thought about things.
Only *me* who really thought about things.
Even though Campy was a poet and an artist.
And Karlos was a musician and a math head.
And Omba was just plain hot. BTW, not being sexist. To me, she *is* hot.
And Mr. Bloom did know how to teach English and get kids excited about metaphors and writing.
And my dad will someday have a home in Moose Jaw, Saskatchewan.
And my mom, well, maybe she will take a course on how to belly laugh.
And, Chloe? She will become visible. Not sure, but she could.
And Auntie Melba and almost Uncle Dewey? Call before you visit and, even then, don't stay too long. As my dad says, guests, like fish, begin to smell after three days. Actually, my dad admitted that it was Benjamin Franklin who said that first.
Also, Auntie Melba, please don't hand wash and shower-rod dry your oversized panties at our house for environmental reasons.
And even slug teachers well, perhaps, and a huge *perhaps,* may have non-slug moments.
Okay, doubtful.
Not sure what the odds are on this but pretty low, I imagine.
It *could* happen, which is a fresh display of my new manhood maturity.
Could.

Coulda. Woulda. Shoulda.

Slugs are there to see.
And experience.
Could be I'm not the only one to know this.
To see this.
Maybe, now, you do, too.

To know that you exist in a world infested by slugs is the key.
It helps to learn how to navigate the slug world.
Know the course.
And to take action, that is key.
Be a person of action, right, Ernest?

Otherwise, if you stand still, the slugs will infest you.
Know, too, that there are others who aren't slugs.
They don't infest.
You will know who they are. I did.

Know that there are others, many, really, who have slug days.
Some more than others.
Hopefully they can return to their non-slug forms.
Hopefully.

I have had a slug day.
Or moment or two.
It could've been one of those moments with Campy on her side porch.
But it wasn't.
But if it had been, I would've had to have come back in non-slug form.
And be a man of action.
Probably an awkward man of action.
I'm sure.

Always remember.
How to look.
How to look at the world.
Look closely.
Always look.
Keep looking.
And experiencing.
And making adventures.

If you overhear a conversation in *Burpese*, that is always a good sign.
Go toward it.

The Manhood

Today, I am in my manhood.
It's the first day.
And I didn't have to take a standardized test to get here.
Okay, there were some tests, though.

I can't wait for tomorrow.
And the day after that.
I am a man.

I am *embarked*.
I know I live in a world infested *and* surrounded by slugs.
But it can't *infest* me with slug slime.
You, neither.

I did it, Ernest, my way.
That was part of it, too, right? To figure it out?
Write a book.
Plant a tree.
Fight a bull.
Father a Son.

I will know the course.
And keep figuring it out as it changes.
I will keep salt handy at all times.
And be a person of action and adventure.
I will keep writing.
And I will learn Maltese.
Somehow.
And also be able to speak it using *Burpese*.

Thank you for what you have shared, Ernest.
On how to live in this world surrounded by slugs.

Is there anything else I need to know?

¡Olé!

Me, Campy/poetry from a quiet corner.

Epilogue: Begin with a poem

Life is not a broken-winged bird.

A Kro can fly—

So can you.

~ Campanella Aminifu Mamolo

Again, Mr. Langston Hughes, thank you.

Me, Campy/poetry from a quiet corner.

Hallways in a Dream

I walk from one era to another down the long corridor
where the tapestry-covered walls were something I didn't recognize.
For some wealthy baron, these, surely, were a valued prize
with jewel-laden double doors beckoning to be opened
as the vast ballroom filled with piano dreams of Chopin.

I walk from one era to another down the long corridor
hearing a mariachi band and notice a handsome *matador*
sitting near a rugged bearded man known as Papa
regaling all with stories at this moveable feast of supper.

Dishes of oysters, fish and crustaceans flavored, savored
and seasoned with tales of courage of the wounded and the braver
in wartime, big game hunting and putting words on a page
and becoming a man through the stages of coming of age.

To meet and hear words of Hemingway, I understood for me
that Ernest was louder than life and that his guarantee
to be a man was to grow yourself and have a plan
to talk and fill your mind from adventures you began.

I wanted to ask, "Do you know how your words are taken?"
But the poet from a quiet corner in me was not easily awakened.
Hard to get a word in edgewise when the stories are never ending
leaving time for my own thoughts and knowing my understanding.

I walk from one era to another down the long corridor
to where I live in lockered hallways and poems with mixed metaphors
and see that something, too, has changed from inside me and out
because yesterday's girl has seen and learned more of what life is about.

~ C.A.M.

Me, Karlos/Math Head/Numbers Poet.

Scrabble as Life*

My life = *music* and *math*
9 points for one, 9 for the other
Equal on my thirteen-year path
Add in my mother and stupid brother.

14 points to be a family
Minus 5 points for my dad
A lot of responsibility
That I wish I didn't have.

14 minus 5 = 9
Add 1 more for the word *friend*—
Kro, the <u>man</u>, underlined,
Campy, her musical words penned.

Does our family stay the same?
Or is it just a word game?

—Karlos Honah-Lee Webb

* You Do the Math!
  Scrabble Letters Value:

A = 1; **B** = 3; **C** = 3; **D** = 2; **E** = 1; **F** = 4; **G** = 2; **H** =4; **I** = 1; **J** = 8; **K** = 5; **L** = 1; **M** = 3; **N** = 1;
O = 1; **P** = 3; **Q** = 10; **R** = 1; **S** = 1; **T** = 1; **U** = 1; **V** = 4; **W** = 4; **X** = 8; **Y** = 4; **Z** = 10

Me. Poet/maybe.

This Is Just to Say

I have found
a potato
chip that was
in the bag

and which
you were probably
saving
for lunchtime

Forgive me,
it looks like Ernest
so crisp
and salty.

—Ezekiel Kro Kandle

. . . William Carlos Williams preferred plums, I think.

The End

No, it isn't.

I wrote a book.
You read a book.

If you have to, and I know it's a pain, good luck with doing a book report, book talk or book share.

Or, doing a book podcast, being part of a lit circle or book club or whatever it is that you have to do when you read a book for school.

And, good luck always.

Especially if you have to do a PowerPoint.

I hope I was of some help.

For a long time now I have tried to simply write the best I can. Sometimes I have good luck and write better than I can.

—Ernest Hemingway

An Homage

This is my homage to the poets and writers who, without even knowing it, helped me with this book. Thank you.

Please go to their original works to read and enjoy just because *no one* is making you do it. Do it for you.

- Maya Angelou—"Still I Rise"

- Elizabeth Barrett Browning—"How Do I Love Thee?" (Sonnet 43)

- Emily Dickinson—"I'm Nobody! Who are you?" (Poem 260)

- Martín Espada—"Advice to Young Poets"

- Langston Hughes—"I, Too" and "Dreams"

- William Shakespeare—*Romeo and Juliet* and his love sonnets

- Walt Whitman—"I Sing the Body Electric"

- William Carlos Williams—"The Red Wheelbarrow" and "This Is Just To Say"

And, of course,

the work of Ernest Hemingway—

There are so many more . . . find yours.

And, always pass the salt.

—Kro Kandle

Acknowledgments

To the non-slug teachers I have had—Thank you and much appreciation for lighting the way.

To the slug teachers I have had—Thank you, too, for that was also an education. Everyone tried and did their best.

To the Readers—
An appreciation and continual encouragement to those navigating through a world surrounded by slugs that may appear in all shapes, ages and varieties. Slugs live in dark places during the day but there is always light overhead. Look for the light. It is there.

*   *   *   *   *

Gabe and Tali—More than there are stars in the sky . . . always.

Diane—Hiking magical trails, climbing mountains, . . .

To the loving memory of my hardworking parents—Esther Shlachter Arnold and Irving Arnold

Rochelle Solomon and Adam Solomon: Cleveland rocks!

Ileana Martinez—Thank you for the longest, continuous school lunch date.

Lori Renn Parker—Your gracious and supportive manner, incisive editing skills and gentle humor are all so valued and appreciated!

Jacob Tobia—Thanks for your guidance in understanding the usage of gender-neutral pronouns.

Derek Donavan—Many thanks to you and *The Kansas City Star* for your helpful information.

And to Kevin Atticks, Shelby Ehret, Tyler Mummery, Alexandra Chouinard and Elliot King—A heartfelt thanks to you all at Apprentice Press/Loyola University Maryland.

Many thanks to the following folks who supported the writing of this book by taking the time to either review the manuscript, provide good humor, supply tech support, be a friend or valued colleague and/or all of the above: Sandy Siegel, Fred Lown, Joseph Tovares, Tom Jefferson, Keith Arian, Gary Pollack, Ari Plaut, Jenna Bjorkman, Lynn Bjorkman, Jon Plaut, Kathy Wilson, Ilene Perlman, Quinn Eli, Richard S. Brown, Caroline Mosca Pease, Marie Lanzo, Diane Coletti, Beth Opiyo, Cleo Syph, Kirsten Turner, Bob Golden, Caleb Cutler, Doreen Vaglica, Sue Riley, Leah Cotton, Miriam Fein-Cole, Ben Fein-Cole, Julia Thompson, Simon Kozin, Karen Packard, Theresa Norris, Alycia Peters, Katherine Batchelor and Brett Becker.

About the Author

Eric Arnold is originally from Cleveland, Ohio, and is now living in the Boston area although he has remained loyal to Cleveland sports teams. Working as the stock boy in his father's grocery store is one of his earliest informal education memories. He completed his formal undergraduate education at Miami University (Ohio) and his graduate work at Boston University and the Harvard Graduate School of Education. Inspired by his experience as a public school educator, Eric has written seventeen children's books including sports fiction, science, biography and humor. He's also written "A Day in the Life" series and books for the *Star Wars* movies. When Eric is not writing, he's either cartooning, drawing, reading, hiking or traveling. He is always working on his slug-detection radar.

Apprentice
House Press
Loyola University Maryland

Apprentice House is the country's only campus-based, student-staffed book publishing company. Directed by professors and industry professionals, it is a nonprofit activity of the Communication Department at Loyola University Maryland.

Using state-of-the-art technology and an experiential learning model of education, Apprentice House publishes books in untraditional ways. This dual responsibility as publishers and educators creates an unprecedented collaborative environment among faculty and students, while teaching tomorrow's editors, designers, and marketers.

Outside of class, progress on book projects is carried forth by the AH Book Publishing Club, a co-curricular campus organization supported by Loyola University Maryland's Office of Student Activities.

Eclectic and provocative, Apprentice House titles intend to entertain as well as spark dialogue on a variety of topics. Financial contributions to sustain the press's work are welcomed. Contributions are tax deductible to the fullest extent allowed by the IRS.

To learn more about Apprentice House books or to obtain submission guidelines, please visit www.apprenticehouse.com.

Apprentice House
Communication Department
Loyola University Maryland
4501 N. Charles Street
Baltimore, MD 21210
Ph: 410-617-5265 • Fax: 410-617-2198
info@apprenticehouse.com • www.apprenticehouse.com

CPSIA information can be obtained
at www.ICGtesting.com
Printed in the USA
FSHW011727301218
54491FS

9 781627 201575